Helen H. S. Thompson

Songs in the Night-Watches

from voices old and new - Vol. 1

Helen H. S. Thompson

Songs in the Night-Watches
from voices old and new - Vol. 1

ISBN/EAN: 9783337265519

Printed in Europe, USA, Canada, Australia, Japan

Cover: Foto ©Thomas Meinert / pixelio.de

More available books at **www.hansebooks.com**

SONGS IN THE NIGHT-WATCHE

SONGS IN THE NIGHT-WATCHES

From Voices Old and New

COMPILED

BY

HELEN H. STRONG THOMPSON

"And the night shall be filled with music"

NEW YORK

THE BAKER AND TAYLOR CO.

1888

Press of J. J. Little & Co.
Astor Place, New York.

TO

H. C. T.

THE STEADFAST FRIEND

WHO

THESE MANY YEARS

HAS WALKED BESIDE ME

WITH A SONG

THROUGH DARKEST NIGHT

PREFACE.

THE nights of human experience are long, "Until the day-dawn and the day-star arise in (the) heart." Happy he who can say, "In the night His song shall be with me," and "I will praise His Name with a song," or, who "Instructed in Song," remembereth Him "who giveth songs in the night," and finds himself "Compassed with songs of deliverance." Then, verily, "Calling to remembrance (the) song in the night," "shall *this* song be sung,—'Trust ye in the Lord forever!'"

The heart may, indeed, sing its songs with the sadness of the nightingale, instead of the joyousness of the lark, through its nights of Darkness, Heaviness, Temptation, Humiliation, Poverty, Captivity, Fear,—even all through the "House of (its) Pilgrimage"—it may sing its Song of Remembrance, with a tear in every note, through Sickness, Bereavement and Death, but "The Song of Songs," and "The New Song," will wipe out the tear. These can only be sung now, in imagination of heavenly choirs, chanting the praises of Him who is "the Light of

> " Sing of His dying love,
> Sing of His rising power,
> Sing how He intercedes above,
> For those whose sins He bore."

But

> " *There* shall each raptured tongue
> His endless praise proclaim,
> And sweeter voices tune the song,"

than the most ravishing notes on earth.
So when we speak of " The Song of Songs," and
" The New Song," we know that we shall only tune
the voice to these when the *Night* songs are past
The sweet singer of Israel does indeed say, " Sing
unto the Lord a new song, for He hath done marvel
ous things "—meaning a song of deliverance ; also
" He hath put a new song in my mouth " (of praise).
but St. John, from his vision in the Isle of Patmos, de
clared, " They sang as it were *a new song before*
the throne," . . . but no man could learn tha
song save they which were redeemed from death
Then, dawns

> " That light which hath no morning,
> That knows nor moon nor sun,
> The light so new and golden
> The light that is but One ! "

IN the selection of these songs, the highest stand
ard of literary excellence has not been considered to
the exclusion of those which have the merit of reach
ing the popular heart ; the object being to pierce
with a joyous note the darkness of the night.

Preface.

The writer returns cordial thanks to the publishers and authors of copyrighted poems, who have kindly permitted their use. A few which have been gathered as waifs, are necessarily used without special authority. Particular acknowledgments are due to Messrs. Roberts Brothers, Randolph & Co., Ticknor & Co., Robert Carter, James Miller, Charles H. Adams, Appleton & Co., and more especially to Charles Scribner's Sons, for extracts from Dr. J. G. Holland's "Bitter-Sweet," and to Messrs. Houghton, Mifflin & Co., for quotations from Longfellow, Emerson, Whittier, Holmes, Stedman, Miss Phelps, Mrs. Whitney, Phœbe and Alice Cary, and many others, all of whom, by their courtesy, have greatly aided the writer, to the use of voices old and new, in this collection of songs.

H. H. S. T.

INTRODUCTION.

It is the dark mysteries of life which try our faith. But there are no absolute mysteries in the world. Mysteries are such only in their relation to our ignorance. To God they are as open as the light. Since he understands them they are explicable. We do not need to know the explanation ; to know that there is one is enough. "Thou knowest not now, but thou shalt know hereafter." There is much that we do not understand now, but a Christian does not need to understand. He can trust where he cannot see. Those who trust God only so far as they can see, do not trust him at all. Faith, like the night-blooming cereus, flowers in darkness. Night reveals ten thousand suns, the day but one. And I imagine that earth is as much more beautiful to heaven by night as heaven is to earth. When the darkness of war or pestilence or some other great calamity settles down on men, the angels count new stars in earth.

"Songs in the night" are inspired by faith in God. We must believe that God is good, and if all good and almighty, surely he will bring good out of evil. It is the mistake both of a coarse animalism and of a refined sensuality, of barbarism and of a voluptuous civilization, to esteem pain the greatest evil and pleasure the highest good. But in God's estimate they are of small account compared with character, which is essentially precious. Its value is not relative but absolute. Its glory is divine and priceless. Too great a price in needful suffering, therefore, cannot be paid for it. Pain is not, like sin, essential evil. It may be made the means of immeasurable good, and hence its infliction is quite consistent with infinite goodness and infinite tenderness. Indeed, in perfecting character, sorrow seems to be essential to its highest exaltation and beauty— " perfect through suffering."

Sorrow is calculated to lead us into a close and peculiar fellowship with God. As it is our highest honor that we are capable of entering into such fellowship, so our highest blessedness is realized in its experience. Fenelon said, " He who has God has all things, and he who is without God has nothing." God would fain give us all things by giving us himself. He would have us share his blessedness by making us partakers of his likeness. The great object of our creation and of all our discipline is to lift us up into this high fellowship with God.

Now sorrow often drives us to him. When prosperous and successful, when our affections are satisfied and our will is executed, we feel sufficient unto ourselves. But when earthly props fall away, when bereavement comes and we wake every morning to a fresh sorrow, when we stagger under some great heart burden, then, learning our own weakness and the insufficiency of every earthly stay, we are, as it were, *driven* to God. We pour out our soul to him so constantly that we form a habit of communion, and have such a consciousness of his presence, such a sense of exaltation in his fellowship that we find a blessedness greater than our sorrow. Then we understand that thought of Carlyle's, that man can forego happiness if he wins blessedness.

David says, " Thy rod and thy staff, they comfort me." In human experience, as in the psalm, God's staff accompanies his rod. And David says, " *They* comfort me." It is possible to get comfort even from the rod. Again the psalmist says, " Before I was afflicted I went astray ; but now have I kept thy word." When he sees the fruit which his sorrow has borne, he can exclaim, " It is good for me that I have been afflicted." Will not sufficient faith in God's love and in his power to bring good out of evil enable us to say, " It is good for me that I *am* afflicted ? " Then with Paul we " glory in tribulations," and there rises a song in the night, though the feet be fast in the stocks.

This great and precious truth—the issue of good out of evil or seeming evil—finds its most perfect illustration in the cross of Christ, the central fact of the Bible and of all history. It is very difficult for us to disassociate the cross from the meaning which has

gathered to it during these eighteen Christian centuries. It is associated with that which is deepest in
our Christian experience and most sacred in our relig-
ious feeling. It has entered into art and architecture.
It has become the most beautiful and significant of all
symbols. But to the ancient Jew and Roman it was
hideous and only hideous. It meant to him all that
the gallows means to us. What would we think, if
we saw a gallows on a church, or one within
wreathed with flowers ? What of a golden gallows
set with diamonds and worn as an ornament ? Thus
would our uses of the symbol of the cross appear to
ancient eyes before the offering of the world's great
sacrifice transformed the cross into the world's great
altar.

But that instrument of bodily torture and death
was made to minister to spiritual peace and life.
That old time emblem of shame has become the
Christian's glory, and the death agonies of the cross
were the birth pangs of a new life in the world. *Our*
crosses are capable of a like transformation; for they
are among the " all things " which we know " work
together for good to them that love God." To him
who has this confidence no night-watches need be
songless.

The books, the poems that move us deeply spring
from deep experiences. The pearls, which in this
volume are strung upon the editor's appropriate and
beautiful thread of thought, came no doubt from
deep, dark waters. In their selection the editor has

been governed not simply by the dictates of a culti-
vated taste, which Mr. Lowell calls " the conscience
of the mind," but also by an instinct of the heart, a
profound and intelligent sympathy with suffering
which can come only from its long experience.
These "songs in the night," having served to cheer
the darkness in which they were gathered, are sent
forth in the hope that they may bring faith and
courage to some who sit in the shadow.

JOSIAH STRONG.

SONGS IN THE NIGHT-WATCHES.

		PAGE
I.	SONGS IN DARKNESS	7
II.	SONGS IN HEAVINESS	41
III.	SONGS IN TEMPTATION	63
IV.	SONGS IN HUMILIATION	79
V.	SONGS IN POVERTY	97
VI.	SONGS IN CAPTIVITY	111
VII.	SONGS IN FEAR	125
VIII.	SONGS IN "THE HOUSE OF MY PILGRIMAGE."	141
IX.	SONGS OF REMEMBRANCE	189
X.	SONGS IN SICKNESS	203
XI.	SONGS IN BEREAVEMENT	227
XII.	SONGS IN DEATH	257

XIII. { "THE SONG OF SONGS" 281
AND
"THE NEW SONG." 286

INDEX OF AUTHORS.

Adams, E. E., 168.
A. J. S., 106.
Alford, Dean, 133.
A. M., 13.
Andrews, 260.
Angelus, Silesius, 167.
Arnold, Edwin, 130, 229.

Bailey, 85.
Baker, Ella M., 134.
Barbauld, Mrs., 274.
Barr, Amelia E., 45, 143, 191.
Bassi, Ugo, 222.
Bates, Charlotte Fiske, 139.
Bennett, Adelaide George, 24, 26, 48, 54.
" B. M." 4, 194, 267.
Bonar, Horatius, 45, 59, 68, 92.
Bourdillon, F. W., 194.
Bowring, 265.
Boyce, Laura B., 66, 85, 104, 211.
Bradley, Mary, 27.
Browne, Sir Thomas, 163.
Browning, E. B., 43, 104, 105, 113, 235.
Bryant, 86, 224.
Buckham, James, 117.
Burbidge, Thomas, 18.
Burroughs, John, 148.
Burton, Henry, 119.
Butler, Frances Kemble, 55, 267.
Byron, 120.

Campbell, Helen, 216.
Carr, Laura Garland, 164.
Cary, Alice, 27, 167, 200, 250, 254, 259, 268, 277.
Cary, Phœbe, 39, 75, 233, 240, 253, 276.

Charles, Mrs., 45.
Chase, Harriet, 165.
Chrisholm, William Byrd, 101.
Clarke, Sara J., 128.
Clemmer, Mary, 207.
Cochrane, W. R., 47.
Coolidge, Susan, 21, 39, 53, 148.
Cowper, 103, 118.
Crashaw, Richard, 273.
Crofts, G. W., 270.

Donne, Bishop, 137.
Dorr, Julia C. R., 232.
Duffield, Samuel, 210.
Duke of Brunswick, 67.

Emerson, 144.

Faber, 84.
Fletcher, Josiah Moody, 100, 144.
Fouqué, 260.
French, Hayes C., 33.

Gale, Ada, 116.
Gannett, William C., 22, 169.
Gerhardt, Paul, 21, 108, 238.
Gladden, Washington, 131.
Glyndon, Howard, 146.
Grange, Olrig, 82.
Gray, David, 199.
Grisson, Arthur C., 138.
Griswold, Hattie Tyng, 254.
Grover, Florence, 184.
Gurney, 88, 275.
Guyon, Madam, 114.
G. Z. G., 219.

Hamilton, Eliza Mary, 249.
Harte, Bret, 9.

Havergal, Frances Ridley, 93.
Heermann, Johann, 67.
Herbert, George, 192.
Holland, J. G., 38, 65, 77, 211, 279.
Holmes, Oliver Wendell, 202.
Hopkins, Edwin S., 61.
Hugo, Victor, 130.

Ingelow, Jean, 74, 192, 246.

Jackson, Helen (H. H.), 156, 255.
J. H. M., 161.
Johnson, Mrs. Herrick, 152.

Keats, 49.
Keene, Mrs. Luther, 109.
Kimball, Harriet McEwen, 91.

Larcom, Lucy, 12.
Leighton, Archbishop, 264.
Longfellow, 10, 17, 52, 74, 87, 115, 118, 128, 179, 186, 198, 242.
Louis, Alfred H., 15.
Lowell, 106.
Lyte, H. F., 72, 129.

Mabel, 93, 161.
MacCarthy, 100.
MacDonald, George, 3, 81, 170.
Macduff, 128.
Mace, Frances L., 13, 275.
Marperger, 66.
Meredith, Owen, 205.
Miller, A. P., 28, 49, 122, 193, 197.
Miller, Emily Huntingdon, 237.
Mills, Mrs. L. S., 32.
Montgomery, James, 263.
Moore, Thomas, 94.
More Henry, 238.
Moulton, Louise Chandler, 172.
Mulock, Miss, 102, 213, 217, 223, 265, 273.

Newman, George, 133.

Ordronnaux, John, 68.
Osgood, Frances S., 105.

'eale Rembrandt, 17.
ck, Julia D., 163.
Phelps, Elisabeth Stuart, 252.

Poole, Hester M., 187.
Pope, Alexander, 269.
Preston, Margaret J., 212.
Proctor, Adelaide, 96, 184.
Proctor, Edna Dean, 244.

Rand, Edward Dean, 13.
Randolph, A. D. F., 20, 151, 197, 233.
R. W. M., 15.
Ryan, Father, 176.

Sangster, Margaret E., 50, 150, 158, 172, 179, 247.
Schmolke, 88, 106, 275.
Shakespeare, 49, 75.
Smith, Alexander, 81.
Spencer, Edmund, 77.
Stedman, Edmund C., 29.
Stilling, Heinrich, 56.
Stryker, M. Woolsey, 66, 99.
Sutphen, Joseph W., 83.
Sutton, Henry Septimus, 23, 37, 60, 201.

Tarbox, Increase N., 266.
Temple, Anna, 55.
Thompson, Alexander R., 10.
Tickell, 266.
Trench, 46.

Vaughan, Henry, 11.
Vernon, Nettie, 29.

Waring, Anna Letitia, 130.
Weiss, Susan Archer, 261.
Weitzel, S. W., 14.
Werner, A., 87, 121.
Wesley, Charles, 137.
Wheeler, Ella, 56, 208.
Whitney, Mrs. A. D. T., 11, 20, 35, 37, 115, 149.
Whittier, 138, 195, 206, 235, 243, 275.
Williams, Sarah, 23.
Willis, N. P., 255.
Winkler, 18.
Wordsworth, 195.
Worthen, Augusta Harvey, 69.

Zihn, 72.

SONGS IN
THE NIGHT-WATCHES.

" *And the night shall be filled with music.*"

" *All inmost things naturally utter themselves
in song. The meaning of song goes deep.*"

" *O sing! sing away! sing away!
Sing, Spirit, who knowest Joy's Giver—
Sing on, by time's Runaway River!*"

" *O holy Night! from thee I learn to bear
What man has borne before!*"

Hark! the stars are talking
With human tone and tongue.

" Courage! for life is hasting
To endless life away.
The inner fire unwasting
Transfigures thy dull clay!"
See the stars melting, sinking
In life-wine, golden bright!
We, of their splendor drinking
Shall grow to stars of light.
Lost, lost, are all our losses ;
Love sets forever free :
The full life heaves and tosses
Like an eternal sea.
One endless living story!
One poem spread abroad!
And the sum of all our glory
Is the countenance of God!

GEO. MACDONALD.

THE NIGHT-SERVICE.

But who shall praise God in the night ? the Night
That stretcheth mournful wings from shore to
    shore,
Till silent lie the singers of the world,
Beneath the shadow.

    ·   ·   ·   ·   ·   ·

It is the night,
And in the Temple of the Lord not made
By mortal hands, the lights are burning low
Before the Altar.   Clouds of darkness fill
The vastness of the sacred aisles.   The dumb
And breathless Spirit of the Night is here
In all his power ; no rushing mighty wind
Of organ harmonies is sweeping down
The shadowy place.   A few short hours ago
And all the temple courts were thronged with those
Who worshiped, and gave thanks, before they
    went
To take their rest.   Then many voices joined
To sing the praise of God ; but who shall bless
His name at midnight ?
                  Lo ! a band of pale
Yet joyful priests, do minister around
The Altar, where the lights are burning low

In the breathless night. Each grave brow wears
the crown
Of sorrow ; and each heart is kept awake
By its own restless pain, for these are they
To whom the night-watch is appointed. See !
They lift their hands and praise God in the night.
Whilst we are sleeping, those to whom the King
Has measured out a cup of sorrow, sweet
With His dear love, yet very hard to drink,
Are waking in His Temple ; and the eyes
That cannot sleep for sorrow, or for pain,
Are lifted up to heaven ; and sweet, low songs
Broken by patient tears, arise to God.
Bless ye the Lord, ye servants of the Lord !
Which stand by night within His Holy Place
To give Him worship ! Ye are priests to Him
And minister around the Altar ; pale,
Yet joyful in the Night.

    .   .   .   .   .   .

                    The Priests must serve
Each in his course; and we must stand in turn
Awake with sorrow in the Temple dim,
To bless the Lord by Night. We will not fear,
When we are called at Midnight, by some stroke
Of sudden pain to rise and minister
Before the Lord. We, too, will bless His Name
In the solemn Night, and stretch out our hands to
Him !

                                    " B. M."

I.

SONGS IN DARKNESS.

" The sudden joys that out of darkness start,
As flames from ashes."

"The setting of a great hope is like the setting of the
sun. The brightness of our life is gone. Shadows of
evening fall around us, and the world seems but a dim
reflection—itself a broader shadow. We look forward
into the coming lonely night. The soul withdraws into
itself. Then stars arise, and the night is holy."

" But Thou dost make the very night itself
Brighter than day."

"In days of darkness were songs."

" The woof of life is dark, but it is shot with a warp of
gold."

SONGS IN DARKNESS.

" Only a signal shown, and a distant voice in the darkness."

———————

NOT yet, O friend ! not yet :
   The patient stars
Lean from their lattices content to wait :
   All is illusion till the morning bars
Slip from the levels of the eastern gate.
     Night is too young, O friend ! day is too near,
     Wait for the day that maketh all things clear—
Not yet, O friend ! not yet.

Not yet, O friend ! not yet :
   All is not true ;
All is not ever as it seemeth now ;
   Soon shall the river take another blue,
Soon dies yon light upon the mountain brow ;
     What lieth dark, O love ! bright day will fill ;
     Wait for thy morning, be it good or ill—
Not yet, O love ! not yet.

BRET HARTE.

WE see by night's sweet showing,
   Grandly revealed,
   What day concealed,
Ten thousand streams of glory flowing,
   That never cease to flow:
   But *only* night can show
What lavish light God is bestowing.

         ALEXANDER R. THOMPSON, D.D.

I HEARD the trailing garments of the Night
   Sweep through her marble halls !
I saw her sable skirts all fringed with light
   From the celestial walls !

I felt her presence, by its spell of might,
   Stoop o'er me from above ;
The calm, majestic presence of the Night,
   As of the one I love.

    .   .   .   .   .   .

From the cool cisterns of the midnight air
   My spirit drank repose ;
The fountain of perpetual peace flows there—
   From those deep cisterns flows.

   .   .   , ...

             LONGFELLOW.

A RAVELED rainbow overhead
  Lets down to Life its varying thread,—
Love's blue, joy's gold, and fair between,
Hope's shifting light of emerald green :
While either side, in deep relief,
A crimson Pain, a violet Grief !
Would'st thou amid their gleaming hues
Clutch after those, and these refuse ?
Believe ! as thy beseeching eyes
Follow their lines and sound the skies,
There, where the fadeless glories shine,
An unseen *Angel, twists the twine.*
And be thou sure, what tint soe'er
The sunbeam's broken rays may wear,
It needs them *all,* that broad and white,
God's love may weave the perfect light.

Mrs. A. D. T. Whitney.

DEAR night ! this world's defeat ;
  The stop to busy fools ; care's check and curb ;
The day of spirits : my soul's calm retreat
        Which none disturb !
Christ's progress and his prayer-time ;
The hours to which high heaven doth chime.

Were all my loud, evil days,
Calm and unhaunted as is thy dark tent,

Whose peace but by some angel's wing or voice
    Is seldom rent ;
Then I in heaven all the long year
Would keep and never wander here.

There is in God, some say,
A deep but dazzling darkness ; as men here
Say it is late and dusky, because they
    See not all clear.
Oh for that night ! where I in Him
Might live invisible and dim !

HENRY VAUGHAN, 1621.

S PEAK to us out of midnight's heart,
    Thou who forever sleepless art !
The thoughts of Night are still and deep ;
She doth thy holiest secrets keep.

The voices of the Day perplex ;
Her crossing lights mislead and vex ;
We trust ourselves to find thy way,
Or, proudly free, prefer to stray.

The Night brings dewfall, still and sweet,
Soft shadows fold us to thy feet ;
Thy whisper in the dark we hear :
"Soul, cling to me ! none else is near."

LUCY LARCOM, IN "JANUARY."

THE birds have hushed their chorus ;
   Stars, through the twilight soft,
Will soon be glimmering o'er us ;—
   The moon's aloft.
Hand in hand, let us hold together,
Through the dark and starlit weather.

The little flowers are sleeping ;
   The sun is out of sight.
God have us in his keeping
   All through the night !
To-morrow let us fare together,
Still onward through the changing weather.

A. M., in "The Quiver."

OVER us, patient and changeless and far
   Shines eternity's star !

Francis L. Mace.

LO ! the marvelous contrast of shadow and light,—
   Of shadows that darken and lights that adorn,
And after the day comes the shadowy night,
   And after the night come the splendors of morn.

And raptures and sorrows through all the brief years
  Keep crossing to weave in the web of our life,
Till another, the greatest of shadows appears,
  To hush into stillness the tumult and strife.

O thou shadow of shadows, the darkest of all,
  Concealing what has been and what is to be,
That liest on life and its joys like a pall,—
  Ah ! what is the splendor that lies behind thee !

EDWARD DEAN RAND.

NO evil ! But behold, how tempest-tost !
  Storms beat unhindered on the good man's head.
Heaven's lightnings shatter, or the early frost
  Falls on the flower he loves, and leaves it dead.
No evil ?—in a world where sorrow sits
Vigilant, jealous ; where a shadow flits
  Darkling beside each shape of happiness ?—
Oh, deepest truth, most literal, tenderest !
  There is no evil. Love is here to bless.
Oh, wondrous transmutation ! In his hand
Who gives,—by his supreme command,—
  The clay is turned to gold, the ill to good.
The lightning is his messenger ; his frost
  Chills not the root : who knows God's fatherhood
Knows he rides safe, however tempest-tossed.
There is no darkness ; in love's light 'tis lost.

S. W. WEITZEL.

UPON the sadness of the sea
The sunset broods regretfully :
From the far lone spaces, slow
Withdraws the wistful afterglow.

So out ot life the splendor dies,
So darken all the happy skies,
So gathers twilight, cold and stern :
But overhead the planets burn.

And up the east another day,
Shall chase the bitter dark away ;
What though our eyes with tears be wet,
The sunrise never failed us yet.

The blues of dawn may yet restore
Our light and hope and joy once more.
Sad soul, take comfort, nor forget
That sunrise never failed us yet.

R. W. M.

KNOWN only, only to God, and the night, and the
stars and me :
Prophetic, jubilant song,
Smiting the rock-bound hours, till the waters of life
flow free,
And a soul on pinions strong,

Flieth afar, and hovers over the infinite sea
  Of Love and of Melody ;
  While the blind fates weave their nets
  And the world in sleep forgets.

Known only, only to God, and me, and the night, and
    the stars :
    The beacon-fire of song,
Flaming for guidance and hope while the storm-
    winds wage their wars,
    Balm for many a wrong,
Dropping from healing wings on wounds of heart
    and brain,
      Quenching the bitter pain :
    Love-star that rises and sets
    While the world in sleep forgets.

Known only, only to me, and God, and the stars, and
    the night :
    Dove that returns to my ark,
Murmuring of grief-floods falling, of light beyond all
    light ;
      Voice that cleaveth the dark,
Singing of earth become heaven, of distant hands
    that bless,
      Though they cannot caress ;

    .   .   .   .   .   .

    While the world in sleep forgets.

Alfred H. Louis.

GROPING blindly in the darkness,
　　Touch God's right hand in that darkness.
LONGFELLOW.

O DON'T be sorrowful, darling !
　　Now, don't be sorrowful, pray ;
For, taking the year together, my dear,
　There isn't more night than day.
It's rainy weather, my loved one ;
　Time's wheels they heavily run ;
But taking the year together, my dear,
　There isn't more cloud than sun.

We're old folks now, companion,—
　Our heads they are growing gray;
But taking the year all round, my dear,
　You always will find the May.
We've had our May, my darling,
　And our roses, long ago;
And the time of the year is come, my dear,
　For the long dark nights and the snow.

But God is God, my faithful,
　Of night as well as of day;
And we feel and know that we can go
　Wherever He leads the way.

2

Ay, God of night, my darling !
Of the night of death so grim ;
And the gate that from life leads out, good wife,
Is the gate that leads to Him.

REMBRANDT PEALE.

.   .   .   .   IF indeed
'Tis given thee to perform so vast a task,
Think not at all, think not, but kneel and ask !
O friend ! by thought was never creature freed
From any sin, from any mortal need ;
Be patient ! not by thought canst thou devise
What course of life for thee is right and wise;
It will be written up, and thou wilt read.
Oft like a sudden pencil of rich light,
Piercing the thickest umbrage of the wood,
Will shoot, amidst our troubles infinite,
The spirit's voice ; oft, like the balmy flood
Of morn, surprise the universal night
With glory, and make all things sweet and good.

THOMAS BURBIDGE.

MY soul complaineth not,
    For she knows not pain nor fear,
Clinging to her God in faith,
    Trusting though He slay her here.
'Tis when flesh and blood repine,
Sun of joy, Thou canst not shine.

WINKLER, 1713.

I CANNOT see, with my small human sight,
Why God should lead this way or that ;
I only know that He hath said, " Child this the path,"
But I can trust.

I know not why my path should be at times
So straitly hedged, so strangely barred before,
I only know God could keep wide the door ;
But I can only trust.

I find no answer : often when beset
With questions fierce and subtle on my way,
And often have but strength to faintly pray,
But I can trust.

I often wonder, as with trembling hand
I cast the seed along the furrowed ground,
If ripened fruit for God will there be found :
But I can trust.

I cannot know why suddenly the storm
Should rage so fiercely round me in its wrath ;
But this I know—God watches all my path—
And I can trust.

I may not draw aside the mystic veil
That hides the unknown future from my sight !
Nor know if for me waits the dark or light ;
But I can trust.

I have no power to look across the tide,
To see while here the land beyond the river ;
But this I know, I shall be God's forever;
    So I can trust.

A H, long the storm, yet none the less
    Hid from the utmost reach of ill ;
And singing in the wilderness
    Some small sweet hope, waits blithely still.

Mrs. A. D. T. Whitney.

I WOULD be joyful as my days go by ;
    Counting God's mercies to me. He who bore
    Life's heaviest cross is mine for evermore,
And I who wait his coming, shall not I
      On his sure word rely ?
And if sometimes the way be rough and steep,
    Be heavy for the grief he sends to me,
      So in the night-time I must weep,
Let me remember these are things to be,
    To work his blessed will until he come
And take my hand, and lead me safely home.

A. D. F. Randolph.

THROUGH black waves and stormy blast,
And out of the fog-wreath dense and dun,
Guided and held, shall the vessel run,
Gain the fair haven, night being past,
And anchor in the sun.

SUSAN COOLIDGE.

UP! Up! the day is breaking,
Say to thy cares, good-night!
Thy troubles from thee shaking,
Like dreams in fresh daylight.
Thou wearest not the crown
Nor the best course can tell ;
God sitteth on the throne,
And guideth all things well.

PAUL GERHARDT.

THE child leans on its mother's breast,
Leaves there its care and sinks to rest ;
The bird sits singing by her nest,
And chants aloud
Her trust in God, and so is blest
'Neath darkest cloud.

The heart that trusts forever sings,
For sunshine lights as on its wings,
A well of joy within it springs,
    Come good or ill.
Whatever to-day, to-morrow brings,
    It is God's will.

R ESTLESS, restless, speed we on ;
    Whither in the vast unknown ?
Not to you and not to me
    Are the sealèd orders shown ;
But the Hand that built the road,
    And the Light that leads the feet
And this inward restlessness
    Are such invitation sweet,
    ·That where I, *no longer see,*
    Highway still must lead to thee.
                        WILLIAM C. GANNETT.

S ILENCE and darkness, solitude and sorrow
    In combination !   Can I cheerful be ?
And wherefore not ?   Since I can voices borrow—
Society and light, and peace from Thee !

I will not waste one breath of life in sighing;
For other duties has life been given to me :
Duties and self-devotion, daily dying
Into a higher, better life with Thee.

ANONYMOUS.

THE little flowers breathe sweetness out
Through all the dewy night ;
Should I more churlish be than they,
And 'plain for constant light ?

SARAH WILLIAMS.

I HAVE a little trembling light, which still
All tenderly I keep, and ever I will.
I think it never wholly dies away;
But oft it seems as if it could not stay,
And I do strive to keep it if I may.

Sometimes the wind-gusts push it sore aside :
Then closely to my breast my light I hide,
And for it make a tent of my two hands :
And though it scarce might on the lamp abide,
It soon recovers, and uprightly stands.

Sometimes it seems there is no flame at all;
I look quite close, because it is so small:
Then all for sorrow do I weep and sigh ;
But Some One seems to listen when I cry,
And the light burns up, and I know not why.
.   .   .   .

.   .   .   .   Oh, do thou feed
Thy light, that it burn ever !   .   .   .

HENRY SEPTIMUS SUTTON, 1854.

O BLACK and bitter night,
   Like that 'round Egypt furled
When sorrow and affright
   Seized all the wingèd world !
A brooding, noisome blight
   Whose dark pall heavy hangs,
Like a phantom in the night,—
   Strikes deep its cruel fangs
     In the heart's dungeon cell,
     Within whose crumbling shell
     The naked nerve doth dwell.

Lone in those darksome mines
   My glimmering taper lamp
No longer brightly shines ;
   Paled by the foul choke damp,
Within these sunken caves,
   No resurrection dawn
Shines o'er the blackened graves
   Of buried hopes forlorn.

Dawn, o'er the mountain height,
Thou, the diviner light,
Come ! end this bitter night.

How long, O God, how long
  Has mortal heart the power
To bear this anguish strong ?
  Is this our earthly dower ?
While we in bondage cry
  Must this our portion be ?
The unillumined sky,
  But mocks our misery.
    Earth doth but echoes throw,
    No light is here below,
    Deeper the shadows grow.

Through blinding fog and mist,
  'Neath pulses throbbing so,
One ear alone can list
  The undertone of woe.
Is that one ear withdrawn,
  And do I grope alone,
Like blinded Samson shorn,
  For the pillars of the throne ?
    Nay : though I tread with thee
    Bitter Gethsemane,
    Still wilt thou comfort me.

ADELAIDE GEORGE BENNETT.

RISE up, sad one, and outward cast
Thy sorrows, broadcast, o'er the vast
Engulfing night. 'Twill soon be past.
The waning moon, a faint, thin horn,
Shows day must surely, quickly dawn.
E'en now, the long twilight
Emerges from the night,
And slowly creeps away
To join the opening day.

Let Erebus thy sorrows keep
Chained in the darkness of the deep ;
They would thy soul in anguish steep.
Cast, ere thy soul in sorrow sips,
This bitter portion from thy lips.
Like morning's radiant beams,
The bright aurora streams
From the low, northern sky,
Toward the zenith high.

Like these bright rays, thou too shouldst rise
Toward the zenith of the skies,
As to the sun the eagle flies.
Thy dwarfed experience leave alone,
Thyself to nobler stature grown.
Up ! wing thy eager flight,
Till, far beyond the night,
Beyond thy shadowy fears,
The glorious sun appears.

ADELAIDE GEORGE BENNETT.

A H me ! the ways of God with man,
No man that lives can find them out ;
Who grasps at things beyond his ken
Is tossed on shoreless seas about ;
Yet in the thickest of the night,
For eyes that see, there shall be light.

MARY BRADLEY.

G REAT God, we know not what we know,
Or what we are, or are to be !
We only trust we cannot go
Through sin's disgrace outside of thee.

And trust that though we are driven in,
And forced upon thy name to call
At last, by very strength of sin,
Thou wilt have mercy on us all !

ALICE CARY.

S EEK not to know
What pleaseth Heaven to hide ;
Dark is the abyss of time,
But light enough to guide our souls is given ;
Whatever weal or woe betide,
Turn never from the path of truth aside,
And leave the event, in holy hope to Heaven.

I KNOW the hand that is guiding me through the
shadow to the light,
And I know that all betiding me is meted out
aright;
I know that the thorny path I tread is ruled by
a golden line,
And I know that the darker life's tangled thread, the
richer the deep design.

BRITISH EVANGELIST.

IT was a day of darkness and of doubt,
Like those which desperate men refuse to live,
And in my anguish I could not forgive
The Fate which seemed to bring it all about.
In gloom I sat and nursed my misery still,
With stolid face toward the pictured wall,
When on my head, and pouring over all,
A flood of sunlight through the window fell.
I moved into the shade and nursed my doubt,
Till through another window fell the light ;
Then the glad thought broke on me, clear and
bright:
That thus God's love would always seek me out.
All darkness and all doubt must pass away,
And every night that falls must end in day.

A. P. MILLER.

"NO light !" we say   - . . .
    Yet still serenely shine the midnight stars,
And there are wonders left us to behold,
If we but think to look between the bars.

EDMUND C. STEDMAN.

WILL it be always night?
    God knows how drear
Is earth's poor trembling light.
    Will He not hear
Each whispered prayer, and note each falling tear?

Will it be always night—
    Cold night and lone?
Shall I ne'er see the light
    From His white Throne—
A glimmering light to guide me, trusting on?

Heaven hath no night!
    It hath no waning day!
But pure and brilliant light
    Shineth for aye.
No weary pilgrim seeketh there the way.

NETTIE VERNON.

OUT of the sunshine, warm and soft and bright,
   Out of the sunshine into darkest night,
I oft would faint with sorrow and affright,

Only for this : I know *He* holds my hand ;
So whether led in green or desert land,
I trust, although I may not understand.

Beside still waters ?   No, not always so ;
Ofttimes the tempests round me blow,
And o'er my soul the waves and billows go.

But when the storms beat loudest, and I cry
Aloud for help, the Master standeth by,
And whispers to my soul, " Lo, it is I ! "

Above the tempest wild I hear him say,
" Beyond this darkness lies the perfect day ;
In every path of thine, I lead the way."

So, whether on the hill-tops high and fair
I dwell, or in the sunless valleys where
The shadows lie, what matter ?   He is there.

And more than this ; where'er the pathway lead,
He gives to me no helpless broken reed,
But his own hand, sufficient for my need.

So, where he leads me I can safely go;
And in the blest hereafter I shall know
Why, in his wisdom he hath led me so.

ANON.

WHAT though before me it is dark,
　Too dark for me to see ?
I ask for light for one step more :
　'Tis quite enough for me.

Each little humble step I take,
　The gloom clears from the next ;
So, though 'tis very dark beyond,
　I never am perplexed.

And if sometimes the mist hangs close,
　So close I fear to stray,
Patient I wait a little while,
　And soon it clears away.

I would not see my further path,
　For mercy veils it so;
My present steps might harder be
　Did I the future know.

It may be that my path is rough,
　Thorny, and hard and steep;
And, knowing this, my strength might fail,
　Through fear and terror deep.

It may be that it winds along
A smooth and flowery way ;
But seeing this I might despise
The journey of to-day.

Or if I saw a weary length
Of road that I must wend,
Fainting, I'd think, " My feeble powers
Will fail me ere the end."

And so I do not wish to see
My journey or its length :
Assured, that through my Father's love,
Each step will bring its strength.

Thus, step by step I onward go,
Not looking far before ;
Trusting that I shall always have
Light for just " one step more."

The British Messenger.

I TRUST thee, O Father, Thy word cannot fail,
But storms are about me, the night-winds prevail;
I'm alone in the darkness; Oh ! lead to the way,
Where I may cast anchor and wait for the day.

I sure must find harbor, or may it not be
The tempest shall drive to a safe open sea—
The winds proving friendly to pilot the way
Where I may cast anchor and wait for the day.

Black clouds are above me, O God, what a sight
The lightnings reveal in their flash of clear light !
Rocks all around me, Oh, where is the way ?
Right here I'll cast anchor and wait for the day.

I trust in God's word, in his love, in his might;
He sees in the darkness as well as the light,
Not a rock in the sea but *He* knows its lay;
I'm anchored in safety and wait for the day.

Mrs. L. S. Mills.

DID not life's darkness dim our sight ;
Its sorrows hide Thine own sweet light,
How much of goodness could we see ?
How much of love that tells of Thee ?

Potter's American Monthly.

WE are waiting, Father, waiting,
Through the long and dreary night,
Watching 'mid the gathering shadows,
For the morning's promised light ;
We are trusting, Father, trusting,
Though no ray of light appears ;
And the night is filled with glory,
Though we see our God through tears.

3

We are gazing, Father, gazing,
　On a sky with clouds o'ercast,
And no sunbeam falls upon us,
　Through the darkness black and vast,
E'en our Father's face is hidden,
　But we know his loving smile
Lights the heavens beyond the darkness,
　And will dawn on us erewhile.

We are bearing, Father, bearing,
　Burdens Thou hast kindly given ;
We are learning to be patient,
　While earth's chains are being riven ;
And the links that bind our spirits
　To their destiny above,
Thou art forging from our sorrows,
　Thou art riveting in love.

We are learning, Father, learning,
　Not to murmur or complain,
Though our dearest friendships fail us,
　And our fondest hopes are vain,
Thou dost hold us by a cable
　With its anchor in the sky,
And we wait, 'mid shattered idols,
　For the dawning by and by.

HAYES C. FRENCH, M.D.

AND so we yearn, and so we sigh,
And reach for more than we can see ;
And witless of our folded wings
Walk Paradise unconsciously.

And dimly feel the day divine,
With vision half redeemed from night,
Till death shall fuse the double life,
And God himself shall give us light.

Lose the less joy that doth but blind ;
Reach forth a larger bliss to find.
To-day is brief : the inclusive spheres
Rain raptures of a thousand years.

Mrs. A. D. T. WHITNEY.

IN God I'll trust
Though all is darkness overhead ;
Though not a ray on me is shed,
Believe I must,
That light still shines behind the cloud,
And though this all my path enshroud,
Yet will I trust.
Yes, ever trust.

Though feeling in the dark for God,
I only reach His chastening rod,

And by that crushed,
Am sorely tried by doubt and fear,
Though Faith sees dimly through the tear,
    Still will I trust.
            In God I'll trust.

Though darkness followed be by storm,
Though on the billows walks no form,
    Nor tempest hushed
For me succeeded be by calm,
Though I see not Christ's outstretched arm,
    Yet will I trust.
            In God I'll trust.

Though human help in time of need
I find at best a broken reed,
    Though I have nursed
But secret foes in shape of friends,—
Though love itself in sorrow ends,
    Still heaven I'll trust.
            Yes, I will trust.

                ANONYMOUS.

SOME souls, cut off from moorings,
    Go drifting into the night,
Darkness before and around them,
    With scarce a glimmer of light,
They are acting beneath "sealed orders,"
    And sailing by faith, not sight.

Keeping the line of duty
 Through good and evil report,
They shall ride the storms out safely,
 Be the voyage long or short—
For the ship that carries God's orders
 Shall anchor at last in port.

" *Thou art my God !* " When I say o'er those words,
 I see a light beyond the night ; and hear
Voices far richer than the songs of birds.
 Mine eyes with happy tears then overswim:
The hearts I have are sweetest that can be ;
 My mind's a cup with love above the brim :
Fine incense circles 'round all that I see ;
 In every sound I hear a holy hymn.

SUTTON, 1800.

ALL is of God ! If He but wave His hand
 The mists collect, the rains fall thick and loud,
Till with a smile of light on sea and land
 Lo ! He looks back from the departing cloud.

God sets some souls in shade, alone ;
 They have no daylight of their own :
Only in lives of happier ones
 They see the shine of distant suns.

God knows. Content thee with thy night,
Thy greater heaven hath grander light.
To-day is close ; the hours are small ;
Thou sitt'st afar, and hast them all.
                              MRS. A. D. T. WHITNEY.

          " YOU have said
That God is just, and I have looked around
To seek the proof in human lot, in vain.
The rain falls kindly on the just man's fields,
But on the unjust man's more kindly still ;
And I have never known the winter's blast,
Or the quick lightning, or the pestilence,
Make nice discriminations when let slip
From God's right hand."

          " 'Tis a great mystery;
Yet God is just, and blessèd be His name !
Is loving, too. I know that I am weak,
And that the pathway of His Providence
Is on the hills where I may never climb.
Therefore my reason yields her hand to Faith,
And follows meekly where the angel leads.
I see the rich man have his portion here,
And Lazarus, in glorified repose,
Sleep like a jewel on the breast of Faith
In Heaven's broad light. I see that whom God loves
He chastens sorely, but I ask not why.
I only know that God is just and good :

All else is mystery.   Why evil lives
Within His universe I may not know.
I know it lives, and taints the vital air ;
And that in ways inscrutable to me—
Yet compromising not his soundless love
And boundless power—it lives against His will."

J. G. Holland, *in "Bitter-Sweet."*

THE clouds may rest on the present,
    And sorrow on days that are gone,
But no night is so utterly cheerless
    That we may not look for the dawn ;
And there is no human being
    With so wholly dark a lot,
But the heart by turning the picture
    May find a sunny spot.

Phœbe Cary.

THE stars are in the sky all day :
    But when the sun has gone away
And hovering shadows cool the west
And call the sleepy birds to rest,
And heaven grows softly dim and dun,
Into its darkness one by one
Steal forth those starry shapes all fair—
We say steal forth, but they were there !

There all day long, unseen, unguessed,
Climbing the sky from east to west.
The angels saw them where they hid,
And so, perhaps, the eagles did,
For they can face the sharp sun-ray,
Nor wink, nor need to look away;
But we, blind mortals, gazed from far,
And did not see a single star.
I wonder if the world is full
Of other secrets beautiful.
As little guessed, as hard to see,
As this sweet starry mystery!
Do angels veil themselves in space,
And make the sun their hiding place?
Do heavenly wings flash as spirits go
On heavenly errands to and fro—
While we, down-looking, never guess
How near our lives they crowd and press?
If so, at life's set we may see
Into the dusk steal noiselessly,
Sweet faces that we used to know,
Dear eyes like stars that softly glow,
Dear hands stretched out to point the way,
And deem the night more fair than day.

SUSAN COOLIDGE.

II.

SONGS IN HEAVINESS.

"Down, thou climbing sorrow ! thy element is below !"

"Then come the gloomy hours, when the fire will neither burn on our hearths nor in our hearts, and all without and within is dismal, cold and dark."

"Who ne'er his bread in sorrow ate,
Who ne'er the mournful midnight hours
Weeping upon his bed hath sate,
He knows ye not, ye Heavenly Powers !"

"Grief within our hearts grows strong
With passionate meaning, till thou come
And turn it to a song."

SONGS IN HEAVINESS.

"Strike ! Thou the anthem, we, Thy keys !"

———

I THINK we are too ready with complaint
In this fair world of God's.   Had we no hope
Indeed, beyond the zenith and the slope
Of yon gray blank sky, we might grow faint
To muse upon Eternity's constraint
    Round our aspirant souls.   But since the scope
    Must widen early, is it well to droop
For a few days consumed in loss and taint ?
O pusillanimous heart, be comforted,
    And, like a cheerful traveler, take the road
Singing, beside the hedge.   What if the bread
    Be bitter in thine inn, and thou unshod
To meet the flints ?   At least it may be said,
" Because the way is *short*, I thank thee, God ! "

E. B. BROWNING.

WHEN the song's gone out of your life,
     That you thought would last to the end—
That first sweet song of the heart,
     That no after days can lend—
The song of the birds to the trees,
     The song of the wind to the flowers,
The song that the heart sings to itself
     When it wakes in life's morning hours—

You can start no other song ;
     Not even a tremulous note
Will falter forth on the empty air ;
     It dies in your aching throat.
It is all in vain that you try,
     For the spirit of song has fled—
The nightingale sings no more to the rose
     When the beautiful flower is dead.

So let silence softly fall
     On the bruised heart's quivering strings,
Perhaps from the loss of all
     You may learn the song that the seraph sings,
A grand and glorious psalm
     That will tremble and rise and thrill,
And fill your breast with its grateful rest,
     And its lonely yearnings still.

NOT so hopeless, drooping spirit,
　　Yon clouds at length will rise ;
And beyond them in the distance
　Spreads a realm of sunny skies.
　　God's promise standeth fast,
　　And the glory breaks at last ;
　　Peace is rising out of strife,
　　Death is dying into life.
　　Up springs the eternal sun,
　　Heaven and earth will soon be one.

　　　　　　　　　　　　HORATIUS BONAR.

IS thy cruise of comfort failing ?
　　Rise and share it with another,
And through all the years of famine
　It shall serve thee and thy brother ;
　Love divine will fill thy storehouse,
　　Or thy handful still renew ;
　Scanty fare for one will often
　　Make a royal feast for two.

　　　　　　　　　　　　　MRS. CHARLES.

　.　　　.　　　.　　　.　　　.　　　.

　　　　　　　I REMEMBER best
　The good time when we were unhappy ; then
When we were full of sorrows and unrest,
　Without a friend among the sons of men,

We found " the Comforter," we found " the Light,"
We found " the Strength " beyond our doubts and
    fears ;
We met with angels both by day and night,
    And touched " the Hand " that wiped away our
    tears.

                                    AMELIA E. BARR.

O UR course is onward, onward, into light :
    What though the darkness gathereth amain ?
Yet to return or tarry both are vain.
How tarry, when around us is thick night ?
Whither return ? What flower yet ever might,
    In days of gloom and cold and stormy rain,
    Inclose itself in its green bud again—
Hiding from wrath of tempest out of sight ?
Courage ! we travel through a darksome cave,
    But still, as nearer to the light we draw,
        Fresh gales will reach us from the upper air
And wholesome dews of heaven our foreheads lave ;
    The darkness lighten more, till, full of awe,
        We stand in open sunshine—unaware.

                                    TRENCH.

T HERE is always sunrise somewhere
        Though the night be 'round thee drawn,
Somewhere still the east is bright'ning
        With the rosy flush of dawn.

What though near the bat is flitting
  And the raven croaks his lay,
Somewhere still the sun-bird's greeting
  Hails the rising of the day !

Let us lay to heart the comfort
  In this sweet reflection found,
That however dense our darkness
  Somewhere still the world around
Dews are glistening, flowers uplifting,
  Wild birds warbling, as reborn,
Lakes and streams and woods and mountains
  Melting in the kiss of morn !

Ne'er was night, however dismal,
  But withdrawn its wings of gloom,
Ne'er was sorrow, but a day-star
  Hinted of the morrow's bloom !
Ne'er was woe, but in its bosom
  Was the seed of hope impearled ;
There is still a sunrise somewhere,
  Speeding, speeding round the world !

THESE saddened years ! These saddened years !
  Pain, parting, sin—so much for tears ;
So many failings that I mourn,
So many loved ones from me torn,

The griefs of others on me pressed ;
Yet Lord, since thou hast thought it best,
I thank thee for these saddened years.

These toilsome years ! These toilsome years !
Whose work like sunlight disappears
Awhile ! The toil of heart and mind
To help the weak, to lead the blind,
To guide the strong with zealous care ;—
Yes, Lord, in many an earnest prayer
I thank thee for these toilsome years.

Rev. W. R. Cochrane.

O WEARY hearts that languish
  With heavy grief oppressed,
Say to your dreary anguish
    There's One who knoweth best.

Our short, scant lines, ne'er measure
    His purpose reaching far,
Look upward through the azure,
    Where shines the polar star !

Adelaide George Bennett.

. . . . On every morrow are we wreathing
A flowery band to bind us to the earth,
Spite of despondence, of the inhuman dearth
Of nobler natures, of the gloomy days,
Of all the unhealthy and darkened ways
Made for our searching ; yes, in spite of all,
Some shape of beauty moves away the pall
From our dark spirits.

KEATS.

GOD lifts the soul or casts it down,
And schools it in His own wise way,
And fits it to receive a crown,
In some great Coronation Day.

Hope cries, " Rejoice ! thou shalt be blest ! "   ·
Faith cries, " Whate'er befalls is best ; "
Come ! drink the sweet or bitter cup,
And suffer on and struggle up.

ABRAHAM PERRY MILLER.

WE, ignorant of ourselves,
Beg often our own harm, which the Wise
Powers
Deny us for our good : so find we profit
By losing of our prayers.

SHAKESPEARE.

4

IN the dusk of our sorrowful hours,
  The time of our trouble and tears,
With frost at the heart of the flowers,
  And blight on the bloom of the years,
Like the mother-voice tenderly hushing
  The sound of the sob and the moan,
We hear when the anguish is crushing,
  " He trod in the wine-press alone."

How sudden soe'er the disaster,
  Or heavy the hand that may smite,
We are yet in the grace of the Master,
  We never are out of his sight ;
Though the winnowing winds of temptation
  May forth from all quarters be blown,
We are sure of the coming salvation,—
  The Lord will remember his own.

From him, in the night of his trial,
  Both heaven and earth fled away ;
His boldest had only denial,
  His dearest had only dismay.
With a cloud o'er the face of the Father,
  He entered the anguish unknown ;
But we, though our sorrows may gather,
  Shall never endure them alone.

We bend in the human frail fashion,
  And sway 'neath the weight of the rod,
But swift in its blessed compassion
  Still hastens the help of our God.

And the sigh of the spirit faint-hearted
  Goes up in a song to the throne,
Such strength in its need is imparted :—
  " He trod in the wine-press alone."

And therefore he knows to the utmost,
  The pangs that the mortal can bear ;
No mortal hath pain that the Master
  Refuses to heal or to share.
And the cries that ascend to the Loving
  Who bowed Him for us to atone,
Are hushed at the gentle reproving,
  "He trod in the wine-press alone."

MARGARET E. SANGSTER.

C RUSH the dead leaves under thy feet,
    Gaze not on them with mournful sigh ;
Think not earth has no glory left,
    Because a few of its frail things die ;
Springtime will bring fresh verdure as sweet—
Crush the dead leaves under thy feet.

Look not back with despairing heart,
    Think not life's morning has been in vain,
Rich, broad fields lie before thee yet,
    Ready to yield their golden grain ;

Autumn may bring thee a fruitage sweet—
Crush the dead leaves under thy feet.

Murmur not, if shadows fall
   Thick and dark on thy earthly way ;
Hearts there are which must walk in shade,
   Till they reach the light of eternal day;
Life is not long, and the years are fleet,
Crush the dead leaves under thy feet.

A S torrents in summer,
   Half dried in their channels
Suddenly rise, though the
Sky is still cloudless,
For rain has been falling
Far off at their fountains :

So hearts that are fainting
Grow full to o'erflowing,
And they that behold it
Marvel, and know not
That God at their fountains
Far off has been raining.

                FROM " THE NUN OF NIDAROS."

EVERY day is a fresh beginning,
    Every morn is the world made new,
You who are weary of sorrow and sinning,
  Here is a beautiful hope for you ;
  A hope for me and a hope for you.

All the past things are past and over,
  The tasks are done and the tears are shed,
Yesterday's errors let yesterday cover ;
  Yesterday's wounds which smarted and bled,
  Are healed with the healing which *night* has shed.

Yesterday now is a part of forever ;
  Bound up in a sheaf which God holds tight,
With glad days and sad days and bad days which
    never
  Shall visit us more with their bloom and their blight,
  Their fullness of sunshine or sorrowful night.

Let them go, since we cannot re-live them,
  Cannot undo and cannot atone ;
God in His mercy receive, forgive them ;
  Only the new days are our own.
  To-day is ours and to-day alone.

    .   .   .   .

Every day is a fresh beginning ;
  Listen, my soul, to the glad refrain,
And spite of old sorrow and older sinning,
And puzzles forecasted and possible pain,
  Take heart with the day, and begin again.

SUSAN COOLIDGE.

TAKE unto Thyself, O Father,
  This folded day of thine,
This weary day of mine.
Its ragged corners cut me yet,—
Oh still the jar and fret !
Father do not forget
That I am tired
With this marred day of thine,
This erring day of mine !
Forget not but forgive.

.   .   .   .

AS on wrecked battle grounds,
  Some black-robed piteous nun
Binds up the bleeding wounds
  When the day's fight is done,
So, stealing o'er the way
  Where garishly has passed
The heated, burdened day
  To wither, bruise and blast,
Night comes in sable dress,
With soothing, soft caress
To heal and sweetly bless.

Sad eyes, which long do weep,
  Hearts heavy, sick and worn,
Praying for peaceful sleep,
  Hands weary, brier-torn,

Feet that for courted rest
  Halt by the sunset gate,
Welcome this dark-robed guest
  And for her coming wait.
Bird of the broken wing
Cease now thy sorrowing,
Night-time doth healing bring.

ADELAIDE GEORGE BENNETT.

RAISE it to heaven when thine eye fills with tears,
  For only in a watery sky appears
The bow of light ; and from the invisible skies
Hope's glory shines not, save through weeping eyes.

FRANCES KEMBLE BUTLER.

IN my right hand I clasp to-morrow's grief,
  And in my left hand is held the present woe ;
No other hand have I wherewith to grasp
  The needed strength and wearily I go
Weighed down by these two loads, and aching sore;
  And sore dismayed, because no help I see ;
And sore perplexed, because my greater load
  Doth make me lean and walk unevenly.

I lean towards my right,—to-morrow's load
  Is so much greater than the present grief;
But lo ! at last, for my right hand I find
  A wondrous strength, a marvelous relief.
God takes this right-hand load ; I need not hold
  To-morrow's woe ; and now my hand is free
To grasp the strength I so much need to-day.
  I grasp it, Christ, whene'er I cling to thee.

ANNA TEMPLE.

B LESSED are they who are homesick, for they
    shall come again to their Father's house.

HEINRICH STILLING.

L IKE a thorn in the flesh, like a fly in the mesh,
    Like a boat that is chained to shore,
The wild unrest of the heart in my breast
  Tortures me more and more.
I know not why it should wail and cry,
  Like a child that is lost at night ;
For it knows no grief but has found relief,
  And it is not touched with blight.

It has had of pleasure full many a measure,
  It has thrilled with love's red wine ;
It has hope and health, and youth's rare wealth—
  O rich is this heart of mine !
Yet it is not glad—it is wild and mad,
  Like a billow before it breaks ;
And its ceaseless pain is worse than vain,
  Since it knows not, only it aches.

It longs to be like the waves of the sea,
  That break from control, and beat,
And dash, and lunge, and hurry and plunge,
  And die at the gray rock's feet.
It wearies of life, and it sickens of strife ;
  And yet it tires of rest.
Oh, I know not why it should ache and cry—
  'Tis a troublesome heart at best.

Though not understood, I think 'tis a good
  And god-like discontent.
It springs from the soul that longs for its goal,
  The source from which it was sent.
Then surge, O breast ! with thy wild unrest—
  Cry, heart ! like a child at night—
Till the mystic shore of the evermore
  Shall dawn on the soul's glad sight.

                              ELLA WHEELER.

TIRED ! well, what of that ?
Didst fancy life was spent on beds of ease ?
Fluttering the rose leaves scattered by the breeze ?
Come, rouse thee, while it is called to-day !
Coward, arise ! go forth upon thy way.

Lonely ! and what of that ?
Some must be lonely ! 'tis not given to all
To feel a heart responsive rise and fall ;
To blend another life into its own.
Work may be done in loneliness.   Work on.

Dark ! well, what of that ?
Didst fondly dream the sun would never set ?
Dost fear to lose thy way ?   Take courage yet !
Learn thou to walk by faith and not by sight.

Hard ! well, what of that ?
Didst fancy life one summer holiday ?
With lessons none to learn, and naught to pay ?
Go, get thee to thy task.   Conquer or die !
It must be learned.   Learn it then, patiently.

No help ! Nay, 'tis not so !
Though human help be far, thy God is nigh,
Who feeds the ravens, hears His children's cry.
He's near thee, whereso'er thy footsteps roam,
And he will guide thee, light thee, help thee home.

. . . .

O SOUL of mine, when tasks are hard and long,
  And life so crowds thee with its stress and strain
That thou, half fainting, art too tired to pray,
Drink thou this wine of blessing and be strong !
God knows ! what though the lips be dumb with
    pain,
  Or the pen drops ? He knows what thou would'st
    say !

TEARS are not always fruitful ; their hot drops
  Sumetimes but scorch the cheek and dim the
    eyes ;
Despairing murmurs over blackened hopes,
  Not the meek spirit's calm and chastened cry.

Oh, better not to weep, than weep amiss ;
  Full hard it is to learn to weep aright ;—
To weep wise tears, the tears that heal and bless,
  The tears which their own bitterness requite.

Oh, better not to grieve than waste our woe,
  To fling away the spirit's finest gold,
To lose, not gain, by sorrow, to overflow
  The sacred channels which true sadness holds.

To shed our tears as trees their blossoms shed,
   Not all at random, but to make sure way
For fruit in season, when the bloom lies dead,
   On the chill earth, the victim of decay :—

This is to use the grief that God has sent,
   To read the lesson, and to learn the love,
To sound the depths of saddest chastisement,
   To pluck on earth, the fruit of realms above.

Weep not too fondly, lest the cherished grief
   Should into vain, self-pitying weakness turn ;
Weep not too long, but seek divine relief,
   Weep not too fiercely, lest the fierceness burn.

Husband your tears ; if lavished, they become
   Like waters that inundate and destroy,
For active, self-denying days leave room,
   So shall you sow in tears and reap in joy.

                          HORATIUS BONAR.

L ATE on me weeping, did this whisper fall :
  "Dear child, there is no need to weep at all !
Why go about to grieve and to despair ?
Why weep now through thy Future's eyes, and bear
In vain to-day to-morrow's load of care ?

" Mine is thy welfare.   Yea, the storms fulfill
On those who love me, none but my decrees.
Lightning shall not strike thee against my will ;
And I, thy God, can save thee, when I please,
From quaking earth, and the devouring seas.

" Why be so dull, so slow to understand ?
The more thou trustest me, the more will grow
My love ; and thou, a jewel in my hand,
Shalt richer be ; whence thou canst never go
So softly slipping but that I shall know.

" If thou dost seem to fall ; if griefs and pains
And death prevail ; for thee there yet remains
My love which sent them, and which surely will
Thee reinstate, where thou shalt thenceforth fill
A place still warmer, and more steadfast still."

Father ! (I said) I do accept Thy word,
To perfect trust in Thee now am I stirred,
By the dear, gracious saying I have heard.—
And having said thus, fell a peace so deep,
What could I do, dear friends ? what do, but weep ?
SEPTIMUS SUTTON, 1800.

R OLL on, O earth ! roll on, and swing
Past midnight, and the morning bring.

Roll on, sad earth ! too prone we are
To dwell among the tombs, and swear
A dumb allegiance to despair :
For all the prophets of the sky,
Foretell, when scarlet sunsets die
A golden sunrise by and by.

EDWIN S. HOPKINS.

III.

SONGS IN TEMPTATION.

" We saw as angels see ; through loss and sinnings."

" For him that overcometh are
The new name written on the stone,
The raiment white, the crown, the throne,
And I will give him the Morning Star ! "

" In the midst of much failure, have the heart to begin again."

" Of our vices we can frame
A ladder, if we will but tread
Beneath our feet each deed of shame."

SONGS IN TEMPTATION.

" Lives in the darkness show
Their whiteness best."

———————

.   .   .   In the throng
Of evils that assail us, there are none
That yield their strength to Virtue's struggling **arm**
With such munificent reward of power
As great temptations.   We may win by toil
Endurance ; saintly fortitude by pain ;
By sickness, patience; faith and trust by fear;
But the great stimulus that spurs to life,
And crowds to generous development
Each chastened power and passion of the soul,
Is the temptation of the soul to sin,
Resisted, and **reconquered, evermore.**

J. G. HOLLAND.

GIVE strength when'er our strength must fail;
  Give strength the flesh to curb;
Give strength when craft and sin prevail,
  To weaken and disturb.
  The world doth lay her snares
  To catch us unawares :
Give strength to sweep them all away ;
  So in our utmost need,
  And when death comes indeed,
Thy strength shall be our perfect stay.

MARPERGER.

WHAT though we grope and stumble in the way,
  The thorny way by which our feet are led ?
Still strive to walk uprightly, and to lay
  Foundation firm for other feet to tread.

LAURA B. BOYCE.

I DO not know the deadly depths within,
  Where lurk my heart's capacities of wrong,
I cannot fathom what I might have been,
  Abandoned to myself to drift along
The seething floods, whose cruel undertow
  Clutches unwary souls, had not the hand
Of the strong Swimmer, buffeting the flow
  Of death, upheld my life and drawn to land.

I only know that from my fatal self
  One who is strong preserved me ! and I owe
My rescuing to Him, who treads the shelf
  Where sea meets shore along this treacherous
      coast,
To watch the overbold, who dare the woe
  Of waters, lest their powers give up the ghost.

                         M. WOOLSEY STRYKER.

THIS shall please Thee, if devoutly trying
  To keep Thy laws, mine own wrong will
      denying,
I watch mine heart, lest sin again enchain it,
And from Thee tear it.

But since I have not strength to flee temptation,
To crucify each sinful inclination,
O ! let Thy grace and strength provide me,
And gently guide me.

                      JOHANN HEERMAN, 1630.

MY heart grows strong,   .   .   .
  Whene'er I feel Thy love, Most High,
  Doth compass me around ;

But would I have Thee for my shield,
No more to sin my soul must yield,
    But in Thy ways be found ;
Thou God wilt ever walk with me,
If I turn not aside from Thee.

DUKE OF BRUNSWICK, 1667.

'NEATH some shadow oft I wait,
    Like blind Bartimeus at the gate ;
Assured that when my Lord draws nigh,
Sin, doubt and darkness all shall fly :
Hence to His cross I cling the more,
Whene'er these shadows touch my door.

JOHN ORDRONAUX, *from* " *Shadows of the Tempted.*"

GREAT truths are greatly won; not found by
        chance,
Nor wafted on the breath of summer dreams ;
But grasped in the great struggle of the soul,
    Hard buffeted with adverse wind and stream.

In the dark day of conflict, fear and grief,
    When the strong hand of God, put forth in might,
Plows up the subsoil of the stagnant heart
    And brings the imprisoned truth-seed to the light.

HORATIUS BONAR.

On finding a Lily growing in the dry bed of a Pond.

. . . .

NEVER on the clear bright billow,
  Lifted from her lowly bed,
Never on a wavelet pillow
  Rested she her gentle head,
Still the torturing, upward yearning
  Instincts of her dainty race,
Bade her from the dull earth turning,
  Rise in purity and grace.
" Mocking every aspiration
  Prone and helpless here I lie,"
This in hours of dark temptation,
  Was her spirit's anguished cry.
" Vain the hopes, the longings endless,
  For a freer, brighter life,
Making me more lone and friendless,
  Wearying me with useless strife.
Let my better nature perish ;
  Nevermore will I aspire,
Nevermore will seek to cherish
  Higher instinct, pure desire ;
On these weeds will gaze admiring
  Nodding in this earth-born breeze,
Coarse, contented, unaspiring,
  Would I were like one of these."

But the sunbeams on her falling,
  Roused from that despairing chill,
And the voice within her calling,
  Bade her *be a lily* still !

Wind-borne from some purer region,
　　Came this testimony free ;
" Fear not, for their name is Legion
　　Who have hoped and toiled like thee ;
Slowly, painfully, thou learnest
　　What thy destiny must be ;
All thine inner promptings earnest
　　Are but glorious prophecy.
Faithful to the highest duty,
　　Hope, yet work with heart and will ;
Thou shalt yet arise in beauty,
　　Thou *shalt be a lily still.*"

Then as to some touch mysterious;
　　Every inmost heartstring thrilled,
While her spirit, thoughtful, serious,
　　With a wondrous joy was filled.
Blessèd hours of exaltation !
　　Memories of such rapture rare,
Saved her from her dark temptation,
　　Strengthened her against despair :
Though no partial friends beholding
　　Cheered her with delicious praise,
All unmarked her slow unfolding
　　Through the long, long summer days ;
Though half doubtful of her mission,
　　Dreading lest her power might fail,
Musing on that dream elysian,
　　Hopeful grew the lily pale.

All its meaning scarce divining
Still new efforts she put forth ;
For the vital moistures pining,
Deeper struck her roots in earth,
Gratefully her thirst allaying
Every dewdrop gathered up,
Choice perfumes from zephyrs straying
Hoarded in her pearly cup.
Once, to let the sunbeams enter,
Dared to ope that chalice white ;
When instantly her heart's deep center
Caught that golden radiance bright.
So she kept her pure corolla
Free from earthly soil or stain,
Till the autumn winds blew hollow—
Till the welcome autumn rain.
Then a little pool collected
Raised her on her slender stem,
And the lily was perfected
Fairer than the fairest gem.

AUGUSTA HARVEY WORTHEN.

THEY only the victory win
Who have fought the good fight and have vanquished
the demon that tempts us within ;
Who have held to their faith, unseduced by the prize
that the world holds on high ;
Who have dared for a high cause to suffer, resist,
fight—if need be, to die.

L ORD, be mine this prize to win ;—
 Guide me through a world of sin ;
Keep me by Thy saving grace ;
Give me at Thy side a place ;
Sun and Shield alike Thou art,
Guide and guard my erring heart ;
Grace and glory flow from Thee,
Shower, O shower them, Lord, on me.

Happy souls, whose praises flow,
Ever in this vale of woe ;
Waters in the desert rise,
Manna feeds them from the skies ;
On they go from strength to strength,
Till they see Thy face at length,
At Thy feet adoring fall
Who hast led them safe through all.

H. F. Lyte, 1834.

GOD liveth ever !
Wherefore, Soul, despair thou never !
Our God is good, in every place
   His love is known, his help is found ;
His mighty arm, and tender grace
   Bring good from ills that hem us round.

Easier than we think can he
Turn to joy our agony.
Soul, remember 'mid thy pains
God o'er all forever reigns.

God liveth ever !
Wherefore, Soul, despair thou never !
He who can earth and heaven control,
  Who spreads the clouds on sea and land,
Whose presence fills the mighty Whole,
  In each true heart is close at hand.
    Love him, he will surely send
    Help and joy that never end.
    Soul, remember in thy pains
    God o'er all forever reigns.

God liveth ever !
Wherefore, Soul, despair thou never !
Those whom the thoughtless world forsakes
  Who stand bewildered with their woe,
God gently to his bosom takes
  And bids them all his fullness know.
    In thy sorrow's swelling flood
    Own his hand who seeks thy good.
    Soul forget not in thy pains
    God o'er all forever reigns.

God liveth ever !
Wherefore, Soul, despair thou never !

What though thou tread with bleeding feet
A thorny path of shame and gloom,
Thy God will choose the way most meet,
To lead thee heavenwards, lead thee home.
For this life's long night of sadness
He will give thee peace and gladness,
Soul, forget not in thy pains
God o'er all forever reigns.

ZIHN, 1500.

O GOD, O Kinsman loved, but not enough !
O man, with eyes majestic after death,
Whose feet have toiled along our pathways rough,
Whose lips drawn human breath !
By that one likeness which is ours and thine,—
By that one nature which doth make us kin,—
By that high heaven, where sinless thou dost shine
To draw us sinners in,—
Come ! lest this heart should, cold and castaway,
Die, ere the Guest adored it entertain,—
Lest feet which slip upon the way
Should miss thine heavenly reign.

JEAN INGELOW.

SORELY tried and sorely tempted
From no agonies exempted,

In the penance of his trial,
And the discipline of pain ;
Often by illusions cheated,
Often baffled and defeated
In the tasks to be completed,
He by toil and self-denial,
To the highest shall attain.

From LONGFELLOW'S " MASQUE OF PANDORA."

IT is one thing to be tempted, another thing to fall.

SHAKESPEARE.

THE past is mine, and I take it all,
  Its weakness—its folly, if you please ;
Nay, even my sins, if you come to that,
  May have been helps, not hindrances.

If I saved my body from the flames
  Because that once I had burned my hand ;
Or kept myself from a greater sin
  By doing a less—you will understand—

It was better I suffered a little pain,
    Better I sinned for a little time,
If the smarting warned me back from death,
    And the sting of sin withheld from crime.

Who knows its strength by trial, will know
    What strength must be set against a sin ;
And how temptation is overcome
    He has learned who has felt its power within.

Phœbe Cary.

TOSSED on temptation's sea
    Lord hear my cry ;
All seems so dark around,
    Still art Thou nigh ?
High roll the billows,
    Fierce is the fight;
Lord, Thou hast left me
    Alone in the night !

" Hush, thou of little faith,
    Cry not so wild,
Know that I slumber not,
    Thou art my child :
And when the trouble comes,
    Bend to my will;
I bid the wildest storm :
    Peace, be still ! "

"TEMPTED in all points like ourselves, was He—
Tempted, but sinless." Oh, what majesty
Of meaning did those precious words convey !
'Twas through temptation, thought I, that the Lord—
The mediator between God and men —
Reached down the hand of sympathetic love
To meet the grasp of lost humanity.
This man kneeling has the Lord in him.

.   .   .   .

Tempted but sinless;—one hand grasping mine,
The other Christ's.

J. G. HOLLAND.

AND is there care in Heaven ? And is there love
In heavenly spirits to these creatures base,
That may compassion of their evils move?
There is,—else much more wretched were the case
Of men, than beasts :   .   .   .   .
How oft do they their silver bowers leave
To come to succor us that succor want !
How oft do they with golden pinions cleave
The flitting skies, like flying pursuivant,
Against foul fiends, to aid us militant !
They for us fight, they watch and duly ward,
And their bright squadrons round about us plant,
And all for love and nothing for reward ;
O why should heavenly God to men have such regard?

EDMUND SPENSER.

IV.

SONGS IN HUMILIATION.

"So shalt thou come to thy reaping, so shalt thou say—
    it is well—
With lips redeemed from the curse, and soul from the
    uttermost hell ! "

"Heaven to win a soul must bring it down."

"A noble heart like the sun showeth its greatest countenance in its lowest estate."

" Hath any wronged thee?   Be bravely revenged.
Slight it, and the work's begun.   Forgive it, and 'tis
    finished."

SONGS IN HUMILIATION.

*"We mount to heaven on the ruins of our cherished schemes,
finding our failures were successes."*

I WILL go forth 'mong men, not mailed in scorn,
  But in the armor of a pure intent ;
Great duties are before me, and great songs,
And whether crowned or crownless when I fall,
It matters not, so as God's work is done.

ALEXANDER SMITH.

'TIS all I have—smoke, failure, foiled endeavor,
  Coldness and doubt, and palsied lack :
Such as I have, I send Thee, perfect Giver,
  Send Thou Thy lightning back !

GEO. MACDONALD.

G ROPEST thou in failure's valley
     Sad, disheartened and dismayed ?
Lest as in the past thy footsteps
     May be yet again betrayed,
Fix thine eyes upon the orient,
     Turn thee from the sorrow's feast,
Till the never-failing sunrise
     Glorifies the darkened east !

B UT all through life I see a cross,
     Where sons of God yield up their breath ;
There is no gain except by loss,
     There is no life except by death.
     There is no vision but by faith,
No glory but by bearing shame,
Nor justice but by taking blame ;
     And that Eternal Passion saith
Be emptied of glory and right and name.

OLRIG GRANGE.

S OFTLY sing the love of Jesus !
     For our hearts are full of tears,
And we think how walking humbly
     This low earth for weary years,

Without riches, without dwelling,
Wounded sore by foe and friend,
In the garden and in dying,
Jesus loved us to the end.

W HEN the sad soul in weariness
Bows low, and knows its own distress,
Nor finds through the extended earth
The happiness pursued since birth,—
Borne down with sorrow and the press
Of a keen sense of little worth,—
In these dear words its woes may drown,
" Whoso is faithful wears a crown."

There is this thought for you and you ;
God's providence is not untrue :
He serves as well who bravely bears
As he who with distinction shares,—
There is a work for each to do:
The soul that uncomplaining wears
The chains wherewith it is enchained,
Is sweeter for the patience gained.

To be exultant, good or strong,
When praised or flattered by the throng—
When circumstance and men conspire
To raise us to a level higher,—

This were not hard ; but if through long
Prosaic years we do not tire,
Can in small things be tried yet true,
This is to live as heroes do.

JOSEPH W. SUTPHEN.

WHAT else remains for me ?
. . . . .
To build a new life on a ruined life.

HOW shalt thou bear the cross that now
So dread a weight appears ?
Keep quietly to God, and think
Upon the Eternal Years.

Bear gently, suffer like a child,
Nor be ashamed of tears:
Kiss the sweet cross, and in thy heart
Sing of the Eternal Years.

And know'st thou not how bitterness
An ailing spirit cheers ?
Thy medicine is the strengthening thought
Of the Eternal Years.

FABER.

HUMILITY is the base of every virtue,

. . . . . .

God keeps all His pity for the proud.

BAILEY.

WHEN all the weary toil with which we wrought
At our life's work, undaunted by defeat,
Falls from the nerveless grasp, the goal we sought
All unattained, our work all incomplete:

Count not God's plan defeated in the life
He gave to us, nor all our toil in vain,
Because we are not victors in the strife :
Who bravely fights and nobly bears his pain,

Wrests victory from defeat. Not what we win,
But what we strive for, doth the Master heed.
If what we sought to be we have not been,
Our striving may have helped another's need.

LAURA B. BOYCE.

GOD'S justice is a bed, where we
Our anxious hearts may lay,
And weary with ourselves, may sleep
Our discontent away.

I HAVE borne scorn and hatred,
    I have borne wrong and shame,
Earth's proud ones have reproached me,
    For Christ's thrice-blessèd name :
Where God's seal set the fairest,
    They've stamped their foulest brand ;
But judgment shines like noonday
    In Immanuel's land.

OH, deem not they are blest alone
    Whose lives a peaceful tenor keep :
For God who pities man, hath shown
    A blessing for the eyes that weep.

The light of smiles shall fill again
    The lids that overflow with tears :
And weary hours of woe and pain
    Are promises of happier years.

There is a day of sunny rest
    For every dark and troubled night :
And grief may bide an evening guest,
    But joy shall come with early light.

Nor let the good man's trust depart,
    Though life its common gifts deny :
Though with a pierced and broken heart
    And spurned of men he goes to die.

For God has marked each sorrowing day,
And numbered every secret tear,
And heaven's long age of bliss shall pay,
For all his children suffer here !

BRYANT.

THE moon was pallid but not faint ;
And beautiful as some fair saint,
Serenely moving on her way
In hours of trial and dismay.
As if she heard the voice of God,
Unharmed with naked feet she trod
Upon the hot and burning stars,
As on the glowing coals and bars.
They were to prove her strength, and try
Her holiness and purity.

LONGFELLOW.

HEART, my heart, be strong !
Thou art shrinking from the pain,
Wilt thou seek a rest from pain ?
Seek rest—while on earth remain
Sin and shame and wrong ?

Heart, my heart, seek naught ;
Naught for self.   Thou art so lonely ?
Christ into the desert lonely
Calleth great souls :—Heart, *so* only
Can thy work be wrought.

Heart, my heart, be still ;
Thou art crying out for love,
Breaking, for the lack of love.
Love abides with God above—
Bear thou here the ill.

A. WERNER.

B LEST, by whom most the cross is known ;
   God whets us on his grinding-stone ;
Full many a garden 's dressed in vain,
Where tears of sorrow never rain.
In fiercest flames the gold is tried,
In griefs the Christian 's purified.

Midst crosses, faith her triumph knows,
The palm-tree pressed more vigorous grows ;
Go, tread the grapes beneath thy feet,
The stream that flows is full and sweet.
In trouble, virtues grow and shine,
Like pearls beneath the ocean brine.

Crosses abound, love seeks the skies ;
Blow the rude winds, the flames arise :
When hopeless gloom the welkin shrouds,
The sun comes laughing through the clouds ;
The cross makes pure affection glow,
Like oil that on the fire we throw.

Who wears the cross prays oft and well ;
Bruised herbs send forth the sweetest smell ;
Were ships ne'er tossed by stormy wind,
The pole star who would care to find ?
Had David spent no darksome hours,
His sweetest songs had ne'er been ours.

From trouble springs the longing hope ;
From the deep vale we mount the slope ;
Who treads the desert's dreariest way,
For Canaan most will long and pray ;
Here, finds the trembling dove no rest,
Flies to the ark, and builds her nest.

. . . .

Oh, think upon that jewel fair,
And heaviest griefs are light as air !

TR. FROM SCHMOLKE, BY GURNEY.

IN a far-away land on a stone it is written,
   Chiseled in characters fair to the sight,
In the place where He labored, loved and was smitten,
   "The way of the Cross is the way of light."

Beautiful words ! forever outsending
   The story of Christ and His wonderful might,
Telling of love to the lowest one bending,
   " The way of the Cross is the way of light."

Beautiful truth, on my life be thy shining !
   Sun of my day and star of my night ;
So shall I walk unmoved, unrepining.
   " The way of the Cross is the way of light."

FRET not thyself so sorely, heart of mine,
   For that the pain hath roughly broke thy rest,—
That thy wild flowers lie dead upon thy breast,
Whereon the cloud hath ceased to shine.

Fret not that thou art seamed, and scarred and torn ;
   That clods are piled where tinted vetches were ;
   That long worms crawl to light, and brown rifts
      bare
Of green and tender grasses, widely yawn.

God's hand is on the plow.   So be thou still.
  Thou canst not see Him, for thine eyes are dim ;
  But wait in patience, put thy trust in Him—
Give thanks for love, and leave thee to His will.

Ah ! in due time the lowering clouds shall rain
  Soft drops on my parched furrows ; I shall sow
  In tears and prayers, and green corn blades will
    grow ;—
I shall not wish the wild flowers back again.

I shall be glad that I did work and weep—
  Be glad, O God, my slumbering soul did wake—
  Be glad my heart did heave and break
Beneath the plow—when angels come to reap.

———

GOOD night, my foe ! not all the wrong is thine,
          My share I own ;
Forgive ! we human know one word divine—
        The sun goes down !

Good night, good friend ! though poor my gifts to thee
        I will not fret ;
The richer thou whose bounty is so free,
        And sweet my debt.

No longer to revenge or to repay
    I strive or seek,
Empty I came, most empty go away,
    Empty and weak.

As one who wakes no more to smile or weep
    Another day,
So would I humbly lay me down to sleep,
    And humbly say,—

O Thou, who hadst not where to lay Thy head,
    As poor were I,
Didst not Thy mercy make for me a bed
    Whereon to die.

HARRIET MCEWEN KIMBALL.

BE still, my soul; Jehovah loveth thee;
    Fret not nor murmur at thy humbled lot;
Though dark and lone thy journey seems to be,
    Be sure that thou art ne'er by Him forgot.
He ever loves; then trust Him, trust Him still,
Let all thy care be this, the doing of His will.

HORATIUS BONAR.

OH ! tried heart—
 God knows !
Not you nor I
Who reach our hands for gifts
That wise love must deny—
We blunder, where we fain would do our best—
Until aweary, then we cry, " Do Thou the rest ; "
And in His hands the tangled skein we place
Of our poor blind weaving with a shamed face—
All trust of ours He sacredly will keep ;
    So tired heart—
        God knows !
Go thou to work or sleep.

MABEL ———.

IN this cruel fire of sorrow,
  Cast thy heart.   Nor faint, nor wail,
Let thy hand be firm and steady,
  Do not let thy spirit quail.
Wait thou till the trial passes,
  Take thou then thy heart again,
For as gold is tried by fire,
  So a heart is tried by pain.

I shall know by the gleam and glitter
  Of the golden chain you wear,
By your heart's calm strength in loving,
  Of the fire you had to bear. ·

Beat on, true heart, forever !
Shine ! bright, strong, golden chain,
Blessing the cleansing fire,
And the furnace of living pain !

FRANCES RIDLEY HAVERGAL.

H OW dark this world would be
     If when deceived and wounded here,
We could not fly to Thee !
The friends, who in our sunshine live,
    When winter comes, are flown ;
And he who has but tears to give,
    Must weep those tears alone.
But thou wilt heal that broken heart,
    Which, like the plants that throw
Their fragrance from the wounded part,
    Breathes sweetness out of woe.

When joy no longer soothes or cheers,
    And e'en the hope that threw
A moment's sparkle o'er our tears,
    Is dimmed and vanished too,
Oh, who would bear life's stormy doom,
    Did not Thy Wing of Love
Come, brightly wafting through the gloom
    Our Peace-branch from above ?

Then sorrow, touched by Thee, grows bright
With more than rapture's ray ;
As darkness shows us worlds of light
We never saw by day !

THOMAS MOORE.

CAUGHT in the bitter net of circumstance
We strive and faint amid each baffling fold,
While careless fingers take or miss the chance,
Or idle with the precious thing they hold ;
And favored darlings of the world look down
From the fair height, by fate or birthright given,
Wondering to see how under fortune's frown
Along steep paths our tired feet are driven.

Carest Thou not ?   Our prized ambitions fail,
Our dearest droop, in dull days shadowed too,
Their young eyes forced to read the weary tale,
While their vain struggles our past pangs renew;
We fain would see, and save, and live, and laugh;
Fain would have honest heart and open hand ;
Ah ! hope and love make but a breaking staff,
When 'mid our shattered dreams alone we stand.

Carest Thou not, O Lord ?   Old age creeps on,
Blighting each lingering bloom we dare to cherish ;
A little while, and the last day is done.
Carest Thou not, O Lord, because we perish ?

Oh, stretch the right hand, strong to stay and save !
 Speak, through wild winds above, wild seas beneath;
Say, despite failing life and opening grave,
 " Why will ye doubt, O ye of little faith ? "

W E ask Thy Peace, O Lord !
 Through storm and fear and strife,
To light and guide us on,
 Through a long and struggling life;
While no success or gain
 Shall cheer the desperate fight,
Or nerve what the world calls
 Our wasted might :—
Give us Thy Peace, O Lord,
 Divine and blest.

ADELAIDE PROCTOR.

V.

SONGS IN POVERTY.

"Who through long days of labor,
And nights devoid of ease,
Still heard in his soul the music
Of wonderful melodies."

"There is always hope for a man that actually and earnestly works."

"A man's a man for a' that."

"What is really best for us lies always within our reach."

"I am the minister of Mars,
The strongest star among the stars!
My songs of power prelude.
The march and battle of man's life
And for the suffering and the strife
I give him Fortitude!"

SONGS IN POVERTY.

" Let us wipe our tears, lift up our heads, and gird ourselves for brave and cheerful toil."

THE helper of his mother,
  A faithful Hebrew lad,
For sister and for brother
  Christ wrought with spirit glad ;
And made that cottage lowly,
  That work-bench by the door,
A labor lesson holy
  To love for evermore.

O sing ! ye tired and tearful,
  What this sweet story saith ;
For all that 's brave and cheerful
  Comes out of Nazareth !

Let serving hands fly faster,
New years new burdens bring,—
Enough ! if like your Master,
The Carpenter and King.

M. Woolsey Stryker.

. . . . . Happiest man among men,
Who, with hammer or chisel or pencil, with rudder
     or ploughshare or pen,
Laboreth ever with hope through the morning of
     life.

.   .   .   .   .   .

Round swings the hammer of industry, quickly the
     sharp chisel rings,
And the heart of the toiler has throbbings that stir
     not the bosom of kings,—
He the true ruler and conqueror, he the true king of
     his race,
Who nerveth his arm for life's combat, and looks the
     strong world in the face.

MacCarthy.

L ET us be patient with our lot,
    And hopeful of the morrow,
Remembering there liveth not
    A soul exempt from sorrow ;

And even should the cruel hand
Of Poverty oppress us,
Its griefs we better can withstand,
If hopeful hearts possess us.

Contentment cometh not from wealth,
    Nor ease from costly living;
The best of blessings peace and health
    Are not of fortune's giving;
A happy heart dependeth not,
    On fortune's fickle treasures,
But rather seeks a lowly lot,
    Content with simple pleasures.

The ways of God are just and wise
    To every living creature,
In every ill there underlies
    Some compensating feature,
And when the lowly feel the rod
    Most sorely on them pressing,
Full often is the living God
    Most lavish in His blessing.

JOSIAH MOODY FLETCHER.

OH weary heart of the toiler ! Turn
    From the maze of doubt and the dust of strife,
And look for once, on the empty urn,
    And the wide-strewn ashes of vanished life,

And then, beholding thy better hope
With starward gaze and dauntless brow,
See the pearly gates which the angels ope;
This is the fruit of the topmost bough.

WILLIAM BYRD CHRISHOLM.

Laborare est orare:
　We, black-visaged sons of toil,
From the coal mine and the anvil,
　And the delving of the soil,—
From the loom, the wharf, the warehouse,
　And the ever-whirling mill,
Out of grim and hungry silence
　Raise a weak small voice and shrill;—
Laborare est orare:
　Man dost hear us? God, He will.

We who just can keep from starving
　Sickly wives,—not always mild;
Trying not to curse Heaven's bounty
　When it sends another child,—
We, who worn out, doze on Sundays
　O'er the Book we strive to read,
Cannot understand the parson
　Or the catechism and creed,
Laborare est orare :—
　Then, good sooth, we pray indeed.

* Labor is prayer.

Laborare est orare :
  Hear it, ye of spirit poor,
Who sit crouching at the threshold
  While your brethren force the door ;
Ye whose ignorance stands wringing
  Rough hands, seamed with toil, nor dares
Lift so much as eyes to heaven,—
  Lo ! all life this truth declares,
Laborare est orare ;
  And the whole earth rings with prayers.

MISS MULOCK.

H E looks abroad into the varied field
  Of nature ; and though poor, perhaps, compared
With those whose mansions glitter in his sight,
Calls the delightful scenery all his own.
His are the mountains, and the valleys his,
And the resplendent rivers.   His to enjoy
With a propriety none can feel,
But who, with filial confidence inspired,
Can lift to heaven an unpresumptuous eye,
And smiling say, " My Father made them all ! "

   .   .   .   .

Yes, ye may fill your garners, ye that reap
The loaded soil, and ye may waste much good
In senseless riot ; but ye will not find

In feast, or in the chase, in song or dance,
A liberty like his, who unimpeached
Of usurpation, and to no man's wrong,
Appropriates nature as his Father's work.

COWPER.

MY wine has run
Indeed out of my cup, and there is none
To gather up the bread of my repast,
Scattered and trampled,—yet I find some good
In earth's green herbs, and streams that bubble up
Clear from the darkling ground,—content until
I sit with angels before better food.

E. B. BROWNING.

IF by our toil another's feet may rise
And climb the starry heights we fain would gain,
Into a purer air and clearer skies,
  Surely our work shall not have been in vain.

LAURA B. BOYCE.

THY gifts sustain
The body's needs, but poverty and pain
Oft minister to higher wants than these
The spirit sees.

Then come what will,
Prosperity or failure, good or ill,
Unknown or understood, still be adored
Thy ways, O Lord !

Christian Register.

NOT all who seemed to fail have failed indeed ;
  Not all who fail have therefore worked in vain ;
For all our acts to many issues lead ;
And out of earnest purpose, pure and plain,
Enforced by honest toil of hand or brain,
The Lord will fashion, in his own good time,—
Be this the laborer's proudly humble creed,—
Such ends as to His wisdom fittest chime
With His vast love's eternal harmonies.

FASTEN your soul so high that constantly
  The smile of your heroic cheer may float
Above the floods of earthly agonies.

E. B. BROWNING.

LABOR ! all labor is noble and holy !
  Let thy great deed be thy prayer to thy God.

FRANCES S. OSGOOD.

SHALL one who does God's image bear,
And shares each day his tender care,
Forgotten live and die?
Did Christ descend the rich to bless,
And turn from sin to righteousness,
And all the poor pass by?

Ah no! with poverty he dwelt,
And want in every form he felt,
E'en to the want of friends,—
To-day, as yesterday the same,
This friend, the humble poor may claim,
To all his love extends.

A. J. S., *in " New Hampshire Poets."*

THE heart grows richer that its lot is poor,—
God blesses want with larger sympathies,—
Love enters gladliest at the humble door,
And makes the cot a palace with his eyes.

LOWELL.

WHATE'ER God does is well!
His children find it so.
Some He doth not with plenty bless,
Yet loves them not the less;

But draws their hearts unto Himself away.
  O hearts, obey !

Whate'er God does is well,
Whether He gives or takes !
And what we from His hand receive
  Suffices us to live.
He takes and gives while yet He loves us still.
  Then love His will.

And what can our will do ?
We cannot reap from what we sow
But what His power makes grow.
Sometimes He doth all other good destroy,
  To be thy joy.
And He our God knows all our weary days.
  Come ! give Him praise.

SCHMOLKE, 1612.

C OME in, O gracious Form ! I say—
    O Workman, share my house of clay !
  Then I, at bench, or desk, or oar,
With last, or needle, net, or pen,
  As thou in Nazareth of yore,
Shall do the Father's will again.

IN Poverty's dark cell I sit,
And gaze upon the heavenly faces,
That bid me to those luminous spaces
Through which at length, my soul shall flit.

WHETHER winds blow foul or fair,
Through want and woe and toil or care,
Still will I struggle up to Thee :
That though my winter days be long,
And brighter skies refuse to come,
My life no less may sweetly bloom,
And none the less be full of song.

WHY art thou full of anxious fear
How thou shalt be sustained and fed ?
He who hath made and placed thee here
Will give thee needful daily bread.
Canst thou not trust His rich and bounteous hand,
Who feeds all living things on sea and land ?
Be thou content.

He who doth teach the little birds
To find their meat in field and wood,
Who gives the countless flocks and herds
Each day their needful drink and food,
Thy hunger too will surely satisfy,
And all thy wants in His good time supply.
Be thou content.

PAUL GERHARDT.

THE Master, ere His work was done,
Breathed this sweet message for his own
As near to death he drew,—
" My peace I leave with you."

" My peace "—but not the loneliness
Nor friend, nor home, nor child to bless,—
But not his scorned and hated name,
Nor yet his poverty and shame ;
These bitter things he knew,—
But left his peace for you.

Beloved, take the gift anew ;
It passeth knowledge, deep and true.

Tender as is the brooding dove,
And stronger than the heart of love,
   Its home—the Father's breast—
   Was left to bring you rest.

                            MRS. LUTHER KEENE.

VI.

SONGS IN CAPTIVITY.

"Dome up, O heaven ! yet higher o'er my head !
Back ! back, horizon ! widen out my world !"

"Let star-wheels and angel wings, with their holy win-
nowings,
Keep beside you all your way,
Lest in passion you should dash, with a blind and heavy
crash,
Up against the thick-bossed shield of God's judgment in
the field."

"God's greatness flows around our incompleteness ;
Round our restlessness—His rest."

SONGS IN CAPTIVITY.

" There went a swift bird singing past my cell—
O Love and Freedom ! ye are lovely things ! "

I SIT upon a cypress bough
    Close to the gate ; and I fling my song
Over the gate and through the mail
Of the warden angels marshaled strong,—
    Over the gate and after you !
And the warden angels let it pass,
(Because the poor brown bird, alas !
    Sings in the garden sweet and true.)
And I build my song of high, pure notes,
    Note over note, height over height,
    Till I strike the arch of the Infinite ;
And I bridge abysmal agonies
With strong, clear calms of harmonies.

.   .   .   .   .

(*Song.*)   Exiled human creatures
    Let your hope grow larger,
    Larger grows the vision
    Of the new delights.

From this chain of Nature's
God is the discharger :
And the actual prison
Opens to your sight.

.   .   .   .

Hear us singing gently
Exiled is not lost !
God, above the starlight,
God above the patience,
Shall at last present ye
Guerdons worth the cost.
Patiently enduring,
Painfully surrounded.
Listen how we love you—
Hope the uttermost,
Waiting for that curing
Which exalts the wounded,
Hear us sing above you—
Exiled but not lost !

E. B. Browning.

A LITTLE bird I am,
   Shut from the fields of air ;
And in my cage I sit and sing
   To him who placed me there.
Well pleased a prisoner to be
Because it pleaseth thee.

Naught have I else to do,
  I sing the whole day long,
And he whom most I love to please
  Doth listen to my song ;
He caught and bound my wandering wing,
But still he bends to hear me sing.

My cage confines me 'round,
  Abroad I cannot fly ;
But though my wing is closely bound
  My heart's at liberty ;
My prison walls cannot control
The flight, the freedom of the soul.

Madam Guyon's "Prison Hymn."

SORROW and silence are strong, and patient
endurance is godlike.

Longfellow.

GOD plumeth many a spirit, still withholding
space to soar,
Bids it wait with folded pinion till He openeth wide
  the door :
Seals a sense that still respondeth dimly to some distant good,
Stirring all the mortal nature with an unborn angel-
  hood.

Mrs. A. D. T. Whitney.

O LITTLE bird ! that all the weary day
    Art beating thy soft breast against the wire,
And singing many a weak and feeble lay,
    Thy song lost in the passion of desire,

O dost thou dream of winnowing the air
    At dewy dawn—untrammeled, gay and free,
Feeling again—oh ! bliss beyond compare—
    The olden thrill of thy lost liberty ?

Thou restless one ! Dost dream of meadow rills,
    Speeding away the daisied meadows through ;
Of sighing pines upon far, lonely hills ;
    Of myriad voices that thy freedom knew :

Of silent nights in forests darkly deep,
    Lit dimly by a pale moon sailing high,
When gentle winds rocked thee and thine to sleep
    With many a softly murmured lullaby ?

Unhappy one ! I'd tell thee if I could,
    The uselessness of warring against fate.
Fold thy soft wings, and, as in leafy wood,
    Sing thy best song, and for thy freedom wait.

Perhaps e'er long, in notes of ecstacy,
    Thy song shall scorn thy narrow prison bars,
And in a burst of rapturous melody
    Seek endless freedom 'mongst the distant stars.

Then all forgotten will thy longing be :
Contented thou wilt occupy thy place :
For thy sweet song, the supreme part of thee,
Will still be sounding through the fields of space.

ADA GALE.

I KNOW a dark and lonely dell,
A forest nook where elves might dwell,
So lost in shade, so far away,
It seems forgotten of the day.

But in the waving hemlocks high
There is an island of blue sky—
A little space, o'er which are blown
White clouds, and where the stars look down.

'Tis so with thee, forsaken heart,
However cold and lost thou art,
However lost to human ken,
And narrow sympathies of men.

Look up ! thou hast the strip of sky;
Thine outlook opens wide and high,
Where loves, like stars, forever shine,
And sympathies are deep, divine.

JAMES BUCKHAM.

H E is the freeman whom the truth makes free,
   And all are slaves beside. There's not a chain
That hellish foes confederate for his harm
Can wind around him, but he casts it off
With as much ease as Samson with his green withes.

    .   .   .   .

His freedom is the same in every state;
And no condition of this changeful life,
So manifold in cares, whose every day
Brings its own evil with it, makes it less.
For he has wings that neither sickness, pain,
Nor penury can cripple or confine ;
No nook so narrow but he spreads them there
With ease, and is at large. The oppressor holds
His body bound ; but knows not what a range
His spirit takes, unconscious of a chain;
And that to bind him is a vain attempt,
Whom God delights in, and in whom he dwells.

COWPER.

H OPE in our souls is king ;
   And the king never dies !

LONGFELLOW.

W ERE there no night we could not read the stars,
   The heavens would turn into a blinding glare;
Freedom is best seen through prison bars.
   And rough seas make the haven passing fair.

We cannot measure joys but by their loss,
   When blessings fade away we see them then ;
Our richest clusters grow around the cross,
   And in the night-time angels sing to men.

The seed must first lie buried deep in earth,
   Before the lily opens to the sky ;
So, "light is sown," and gladness has its birth,
   In the dark deeps where we can only cry.

    .   .   .   .   ,   .

Come then, my soul, be brave to bear ;
   Thy life is bruised that it may be more sweet ;
The cross will soon be left, the crown we'll wear;
   Nay, we will cast it at our Saviour's feet.

HENRY BURTON.

HOMEWARD the swift-winged seagull takes its
    flight,
   The ebbing tide breaks softly on the sand ;
The sunlit boats draw shoreward for the night ;
   The shadows deepen over sea and land ;
Be still, my soul, thine hour shall also come ;
Behold, one evening God shall lead thee home.

THE earth, O prisoned soul, is thine.
Rise up ! come forth ! in sun and air
Claim and possess thy rightful share.
Come forth ! in love and life divine,
Thou child of God ! the world is thine.

IN weariness I wait and pray,
As waits the restless for the day :
Watching the still starlight !
As waits the soldier in reserve,
While longing stirs through every nerve !

This hour in patience let me wait.
Dawn comes not premature or late.
Then better far than I have sought,
And better far than I have thought,
God *will* give what is best.

ETERNAL spirit of the chainless mind !
Brightest in dungeons, Liberty ! thou art,
For there thy habitation is the heart.

BYRON.

O H, our Father, our Father,
Hearest Thou not our pain ?
We can only cry as the young birds cry,
Again, and yet again ;
Blind, and helpless, and almost mad,
And shall our crying be vain ?

Oh ! our Father, our Father,
We have heard them speak of Thee,
But our eyes are dim and our hearts are dull,
And we know not if Thou be—
The yoke-bound neck, and the fettered hand,
Bowed to the dust are we.

Oh ! our Father, our Father,
Dwelling in love and light !
There is none to guide us, or hear our cry.
In the weary, pathless night,
Earth is burdened with cruel wrong—
Wilt thou not do us right ?

A. WERNER, *in " The King of the Silver City."*

I S not the night all dark, and murky with vapors
of Death ?
Stars there are none to see, and the rank mist chokes
our breath,

And the chains have cut to the soul. Nay now—
    have we souls at all ?   .
All man's glories stripped from us—have we yet
    lower to fall ?   .   .   .
Since we have no sunrise, no moon nor stars to
    shine !

Listen, O helpless and weary ! the time is coming—
    but wait !—
Lift up your eyes in hope to the heaven's eastern
    gate !—
It shall glow with gold anon,—and *then there is*
    work for you !   .   .   .

                  A. W., *in Cambridge Review.*

.   .   .   .   BEHOLD the throng
Of wounded souls that bear some gloomy wrong.
Ah ! sorrowing friend, what multitudes to-day
Walk by thy side, unknown, the thorny way,
And walk in darkness, praying for the light,
Like one who walks his chamber in the night,
And ever through the window looks away
Into the chilly night, and longs for day !
    .   .   .   .   .   .

One . . source remains to soothe thy breast,
The one great comfort which includes the rest :
Submit thy sorrow and thy soul to God,
And learn what peace it is to kiss His rod,
Who answers wishes ere they turn to prayers
And with his blessing takes us unawares—
Who girds us, though we know Him not, and stands
Above us always with his helping hands.
As when a little child, returned from play,
Finds the door closed and latched across its way,
Against the door, with infant push and strain,
It gathers all its strength and strives in vain ;—
Unseen within, a loving father stands,
And lifts the iron latch with easy hands ;
Then, as he lightly draws the door aside,
He hides behind it, while, with baby pride
And face aglow, in struts the little one,
Flushed and rejoiced to think what it has done !
So, when men find across life's rugged way
Strong doors of trouble, barred from day to day,
And strive with all their power of knees and hands,
Unseen within, their Heavenly Father stands,
And lifts each iron latch, while men pass through,
Flushed and rejoiced to think what they can do.

ABRAHAM PERRY MILLER.

SHUT in with tears that are spent in vain,
Shut in with the dull companionship of pain;
Shut in with the changeless days and hours,
And the bitter knowledge of failing powers.

Shut in with dreams of days gone by,
With buried joys that are born to die;
Shut in with hopes that have lost their zest,
And leave but a longing after rest.

Shut in with a trio of angels sweet,
Patience and grace all pain to meet,
And faith that can suffer, and stand and wait,
And lean on the promises strong and great.

"UNTO the hills I lift mine eyes,"
And following them I seek the skies
To which they point and seem to say
Christ is our strength by night as day.

I take the lesson to my heart.
Dear Lord, let me not grow apart
From that sweet faith which bids hope rise
And like those mountains seek the skies,
Where thou dost dwell in all thy might,
To guard thy people day and night.

"Unto the hills," yes, unto Thee
Mine eyes shall turn most hopefully.
For hills and walls shall crumble, Lord,
But they who rest upon Thy word
Shall stand secure, and know Thee true,
Though skies of life be gray or blue.

VII.

SONGS IN FEAR.

" He has not learned the lesson of a life who does not
every day surmount a fear."

" Write on your doors the saying, wise and old,
' Be bold ! be bold !' and everywhere ' Be bold !'"

" Go forth and meet the shadowy future without fear,
and with a manly heart."

" Let not your heart be troubled, neither let it be
afraid !"

SONGS IN FEAR.

"Go and dare before you die!"

" Our valors are our best gods."

'TIS the bold who win the race,
Whether for gold, or love, or name;
'Tis the true ones always face
Dangers and trials, and win a place,
A niche in the fane of fame.

WORKMAN of God, oh, lose not heart !
But learn what God is like ;
And in the darkest battle-field,
Thou shalt know where to strike.

" SONGS OF DEVOTION."

GO breathe it in the ear
Of all who doubt and fear,
And say to them, " Be of good cheer ! "

LONGFELLOW.

THERE is a grandeur in the soul that dares
To live out all the life God lit within ;
That battles with the passions hand to hand,
And wears no mail, and hides behind no shield ;
That plucks its joy in the shadow of death's wing,
That drains with one deep draught the wine of life,
And that with fearless foot and heaven-turned eyes,
May stand upon a dizzy precipice,
High over the abyss of ruin and not fall.

SARA J. CLARKE.

PLAN not, nor scheme, but calmly wait ;
His choice is best,
While blind and erring is thy sight ;
His wisdom sees and judges right ;
So trust and rest.

Strive not, nor struggle ; thy poor might
Can never wrest
The meanest thing to serve thy will ;
All power is His alone ; be still,
And trust and wait.

What dost thou féar ?   His wisdom reigns
    Supreme, confessed ;
His power is infinite ; His love
Thy deepest, fondest dreams above ;
    So trust and rest.

MACDUFF.

WHAT foe can injure me ?
  Why bid me like a bird
Before the fowler flee ?
The Lord is on His heavenly throne,
And He will shield and save His own.

H. F. LYTE,.

STRONG are the mountains, Lord, but stronger
    Thou !
Where beats the tempest on the hither side,
Beneath their shelter bloom the vine and rose ;
  So do Thy choosen ones in Thee abide,
Nor fear the storm-wind though it wildly blows,
All undisturbed in their secure repose.

OUR very perils shut us in,
　　To thy supporting care;
We venture on the awful deep,
　And find our courage there.

Oh, there are heavenly heights to reach
　In many a fearful place
Where the poor timid heir of God
　Lies blindly on his face ;

Lies languishing for life divine
　That he shall never see
Till he go forward at Thy sign
　And trust himself to Thee.

ANNA LETITIA WARING.

WHEN sins and follies long forgot
　　Upon thy tortured conscience prey,
Oh, come to God, and fear Him not :
　His love shall sweep them all away;
　Pains of hell at look of His
　Change to calm content and bliss.

LET us be like the bird, one instant lighted
　　Upon a twig that swings ;
He feels it yield, but sings on unaffrighted,
　Knowing he has his wings.

VICTOR HUGO, Tr. by EDWIN ARNOLD.

DOWN to the borders of the silent land
He goes with halting feet :
He dares not trust ; he cannot understand
The blessedness complete,
That waits for God's beloved at His right hand.

He dreads to see God's face ; for though the pure
Beholding Him are blest,
Yet in His sight no evil shall endure ;
So still, with fear oppressed,
He looks within and cries, " Who can be sure ? "

The world beyond is strange : the golden streets,
The palaces so fair,
The seraphs singing in the shining seats —
The glory everywhere;
And to his soul he solemnly repeats

The visions of the book. " Alas ! " he cries,
" That world is all too grand ;
Among those splendors and those majesties
I would not dare to stand :
For me, a lowlier heaven would well suffice ! "

Yet faithful in his lot this saint hath stood
Through service and through pain ;
The Lord Christ he has followed, doing good ;
Sure, dying must be gain
To one who, living, hath done what he could.

The light is fading in the tired eyes,
  The weary race is run ;
Not as the victor that doth seize the prize,
  But as the fainting one
He nears the verge of the eternities.

And now the end has come, and now he sees
  The happy, happy shore ;
Oh fearful, faint, distrustful soul, are these
  The things thou feard'st before,
The awful majesties that spoiled thy peace ?

This land is home ; no stranger art thou here ;
  Sweet and familiar words
From voices silent long salute thine ear ;
  And winds and songs of birds
And bees and blooms and sweet perfumes are near.

The seraphs—they are men of kindly mien ;
  The gems and robes—but signs
Of minds all radiant, and of hearts washed clean ;
  The glory—such as shines
Wherever faith or hope or love is seen.

And thee, O doubting child ! the Lord of grace
  Whom thou didst fear to see—
He knows thy sin—but look upon his face !
  Doth it not shine on thee
With a great light of love that fills the place ?

Oh, happy soul, be thankful now and rest !
　Heaven is a goodly land ;
And God is love ; and those He loves are blest.
　Now thou dost understand
The least thou hast is better than the best

That thou did'st hope for : now upon thine eyes
　The new life opens fair;
Before thy feet the blessed journey lies
　Through homelands everywhere ;
And heaven to thee is all a sweet surprise.

WASHINGTON GLADDEN.

L EAVE God to order all thy ways,
　And hope in Him what'er betide;
Thou'lt find Him in the evil days
　An all-sufficient strength and guide ;
Who trusts in God's unchanging love,
Builds on a rock that naught can move.

GEORGE NEWMAN.

B E not amazed at life.　'Tis still
　The mode of God with his elect,
Their hopes exactly to fulfill,
　In times and ways they least expect.

DEAN ALFORD.

"I TREMBLE at the thought of heaven,"
   She said.   He wondered why.
"At heaven ! whose glories make us glad,
   And more than glad to die ? "—
He asked her, puzzled, half displeased.
   Her dreamy eyes, along
The distant hills looked forth : "I know,"
   She said, "the raptured song
That holy souls have tried to make
   Of heaven ; how they say,
'Thou hast no shore, fair ocean,
   Thou hast no time, bright day ;
With jasper glow thy bulwarks,
   Thy streets with emeralds blaze,
The sardius and the topaz
   Unite in thee their rays,'—
               I know——

"But I, who am no saint inspired,
   But I, who never had
More than a common life to live,
   Nor much to make me glad,
Nor grand experiences that dig
   Deep channels in the soul,
How shall I bear this heaven's vast
   Ecstatic, perfect whole ?
Perfection ! I cannot conceive
   Perfection, and I *fear*—
You see, I could not take it in,
   Because, I'm so used here

To tempered pleasures and small flaws
In all my dearest things,
That to its full capacity
Joy in me never swings.
What if the splendid, perfect heaven
Found me thus lacking ; such
I could not comprehend it all,
And could not bear so much !
Like this, maybe :—a man born deaf
Hears suddenly ; and lo !
The first breath in the world of sound
His opened ears shall know,
Comes thrilling from an orchestra
Perfect ! Oh, yes !—and yet,
The man might swoon beneath the shock
His startled nerves have met.
I am afraid !"

" I thank you, for that word," he said ;
" There is another sense ;
We miss it (so I think), always,
Until we do go hence.
We know there is another power,
Though not whether its tense
Is that we *might have*, or *shall have*,
This unknown sense, from whence
We hope as great things, surely,
As the kitten ten days old,
When her blind eyes, finding their **use**,
To light delayed, unfold.

And so perhaps, this dormant sense,
    Not needed until then,
May be the very thing vouchsafed
    To bear the glory, when
The righteous in the kingdom shine,
    And He, in garments white
Sits on the throne, whom none can see
    And live, to bear the sight.
Eye hath not seen, ear hath not heard,
    Those things he doth prepare.
Perhaps, because, until that sense,
    The look they could not bear.
Eye hath not seen, ear hath not heard—
    Oh, no ! not yet, not yet,—
But rest ; but wait ; anticipate ;
    And, waiting, do not let
Thy heart be troubled ! The man, deaf,
    Not at the sound would start
And marvel, but the new found *sense ;*
    The faculty, his heart
Would fill with joy unspeakable.
    And on its own strong wings
He would be borne above himself,
    Above all lesser things.
The hospitality of heaven
    Will not make earth's mistakes.
When a tired, timid woman, strange,
    Upon that threshold wakes,
It will not be with blare of full
    Processionals they meet

And honor her. With tender touch,
   Tones very low and sweet,
Ways home-like she can understand,
   As if before, there, she had been.
I think they will come softly forth
   And silent lead her in,—
And lead her in, to see the face
   That anywhere would be
The one thing making heaven home,
   Heaven to you, to me."

                              ELLA M. BAKER.

I HAVE a sin of fear, that when I've spun
   My last thread, I shall perish on the shore :
But swear by Thyself, that at my death Thy sun
   Shall shine as heretofore,
And having done that, ...
   I fear no more.

                              BISHOP DONNE.

SEE the Lord, thy keeper, stand
      Omnipotently near ;
Lo ! He holds thee by thy hand,
   And banishes thy fear ;

Shadows with His wings thy head ;
Guards from all impending harms ;
Round thee and beneath are spread
The everlasting arms.

CHARLES WESLEY.

WHY that look of dark dismay ?
Know ye not that God is near—
That thy God doth guard thy way ?
Hast forgot His kind assurance—
He will strengthen, He will guide ?
Art thou lacking in endurance ?
Art thou falling from His side ?
.   .   .   .   He hath told thee
Thou art His, and He is thine,
That His right hand shall uphold thee,
Dost ask more of God divine ?
Oh, then onward ! do not fear,
Ne'er forget that He is near.

ARTHUR C. GRISSOM.

I KNOW not what the future hath
Of marvel or surprise,
Assured alone that life and death
His mercy underlies.

And if my heart and flesh are weak
To bear an untried pain,
The bruisèd reed He will not break
But strengthen and sustain.

WHITTIER.

WHAT a strange Being holds me in his might,
And must forever have his way with me !
Oh ! what if *fear* should, after all, be right ?
Then what a terror nearing God must be !
With such unfailing gifts of life and light,
Why should I dread the Giver's self to see ?

I went my daily ways thus questioning,
My foremost care a cagèd soul of song
That met me always with a frightened wing,
As fearing I had come to do it wrong.
Often I said : " How passing strange a thing,
When I have fed its little life so long ! "

But lo ! a marvel even greater yet,
The timid creature, wildly beating first,
Sank, on a sudden, close as it could get,
And still,—as though its very heart had burst;
While on my own such steadfast eyes were set
As dared me, in their trust, to do my worst.

Between the bars was thrust its ventured breast,
 Whose plumy, golden curve now hardly stirred ;
Then was my long pent tenderness expressed
 In touches like the softest whispered word.
Ah, life-long trembler, needlessly distressed,
 Me and my love you know at last, poor bird !

A new and grateful joy ran through my heart,
 And wet my unsealed eyes like any woe ;
But with what rapture fell my lips apart :
 " I thank thee, Father, I have learned Thee so !
As I, to this frail thing, to me *Thou* art,
 And through my own, the heart of God I know !

CHARLOTTE FISKE BATES.

VIII.

SONGS IN "THE HOUSE OF MY PILGRIMAGE."

" Make the house where gods may dwell
   Beautiful, entire and clean."

" Whatsoever road I take, joins the highway
   That leads to Thee ! "

" Rest is not quitting this busy career,
   Rest is the fitting of self to one's sphere."

SONGS IN THE HOUSE OF MY PIL-GRIMAGE.

" There's a song in the air, there's a star in the sky."

O PEN the western gate,
    And let the daylight go,
In pomp of royal state
    In rose and amber glow.
It is so late, so late,
    The birds sing sweet and low,
Open the western gate,
    And let the daylight go.

Lay down thy daily toil,
    Glad of thy labor done,
Glad of the night's assoil,
    Glad of thy wages won ;
With hearts that fondly wait,
    With grateful hearts aglow,
Pray at the western gate
    And let the daylight go.

Pray at the eastern gate
For all the day can ask ;
Pray at the western gate,
Holding thy finished task.
It waxeth late, so late,
The night falls cold and gray ;
But through life's western gate
Dawns life's eternal day.

AMELIA E. BARR.

A S the bird trims her to the gale
I trim myself to the storm of time,
I man the rudder, reef the sail,
Obey the voice at eve, obeyed at prime,
Lowly, faithful, banish fear,
Right onward, drive unharmed,
The port well worth the cruise is near,
And every wave is charmed.

EMERSON.

W E should live as if expecting
To be angels by-and-by,
Every moment recollecting
The immortal life on high,

Where in purity and glory,
  The angelic throngs above,
Hymn the never-ending story
  Of the great Creator's love.

We should live for something higher
  Than to grovel here for gold,
And to holiness aspire,
  Like the sainted ones of old ;
We should live in the endeavor
  Human passions to control,
And to hold the truth forever
  As the anchor of the soul.

We should live for one another,
  For humanity and right,
True to God and to each other,
  And the soul's divinest light ;
We should live for those in sorrow,
  On the waves of trouble cast,
With an ever firm endeavor
  To be faithful to the last.

In the narrow path of duty,
  In the shining path of love,
In the purity and beauty
  Of angelic life above ;

Every moment recollecting
The immortal life on high,
We should live as if expecting
To be angels by-and-by.

Josiah Moody Fletcher.

A H ! for the heart that goes
Unbenisoned to its rest !
Ah ! for the bird that knows
No mate in its lonely nest ;
Not even the kindly fluttering
By night of a passing wing,
Only the wind's low muttering,
And no other friendly thing.

Shall I sicken of faring apart ?
Shall I die of keeping alone ?
And of bruising my living heart
On the cold unanswering stone ?

.   .   .   .

There is a little rift
Of blue above the roofs,
And away in its peaceful lift,
There are stars that shine like proofs

That I shall not miss the folding
Of God's arms warm about
The lone life he is holding
Safe in the dark of doubt!

HOWARD GLYNDON.

ONE summer day, to a young child, I said,
 "Write to thy mother, boy." With earnest face
And laboring fingers all unused to trace
The mystic characters, he bent his head
(That should have danced amid the flowers instead)
 Over the blurred page for a half-hour's space :
 Then with a sigh that burdened all the place
Cried, " Mamma knows ! " and out to sunshine sped.

O soul of mine, when tasks are hard and long,
And life so crowds thee with its stress and strain
 That thou, half fainting, art too tired to pray,—
Drink thou this wine of blessing and be strong !
God knows ! What though the lips be dumb with
 pain,
Or the pen drops ? He knows what thou would'st
 say.

WHY should we do ourselves this wrong,
 Or others,—that we are not always strong—

That we are ever overborne with care,
That we should ever weak or heartless be,
Anxious or troubled, while with us is prayer,
    And joy and strength and courage are with Thee?

                        Lo! amid the press,
    The whirl and hum and pressure of my day,
I hear Thy garment's sweep, Thy seamless dress,
And close beside my work and weariness,
    Discern Thy gracious form, not far away,
But very near, O Lord! to help and bless.

The busy fingers fly, the eyes may see
    Only the glancing needle which they hold,
But all my life is blossoming inwardly,
And every breath is like a litany ;
    While through each labor, like a thread of gold,
Is woven the sweet consciousness of Thee !

                                SUSAN COOLIDGE.

SERENE, I fold my hands and wait,
    Nor care for wind, nor tide, nor sea ;
I rave no more 'gainst time or fate,
    For lo ! mine own shall come to me.

What matter if I stand alone ?
I wait with joy the coming years :
My heart shall reap where it has sown,
And garner up its fruit of tears.

JOHN BURROUGHS.

A MONG so many can He care ?
Can special love be everywhere ?
A myriad homes—a myriad ways,—
And God's eye over every place ?

Over; but in ? The world is full,
A grand Omnipotence must rule ;
But is there life that doth abide
With mine own, living side by side ?

So many and so wide abroad :
Can any heart have all of God ?
From the great spaces, vague and dim,
May one small household gather him ?—

I asked ; my soul bethought of this :—
" In just that very place of His
Where He hath put and keepeth you,
God hath no other thing to do."

MRS. A. D. T. WHITNEY.

LORD ! if I dip my cup into the sea,
It rises full ! Such cup each soul may be,
Such ocean is Thy good !

SOMETIMES I am tempted to murmur
That life is flitting away,
With only a round of trifles
Filling each busy day ;
Dusting nooks and corners,
Making the house look fair,
And patiently taking on me
The burden of woman's care.

Comforting childish sorrows,
And charming the childish heart
With the simple song and story,
Told with a mother's art ;
Setting the dear home table,
And clearing the meal away,
And going on little errands
In the twilight of the day.

One day is just like another !
Sewing and piecing well
Little jackets and trousers,
So neatly that none can tell

Where are the seams and joinings.
Ah ! the seamy side of life
Is kept out of sight by the magic
Of many a mother and wife !

And oft when ready to murmur
That life is flitting away,
With the self-same round of duties
Filling each busy day,
It comes to my spirit sweetly
With the grace of a thought divine :
" You are living, toiling, for love's sake,
And the loving should never repine.

" You are guiding the little footsteps
In the way they ought to walk ;
You are dropping a word for Jesus
In the midst of your household talk ;
Living your life for love's sake
Till the homely cares grow sweet,
And sacred the self-denial
That is laid at the Master's feet."

MARGARET E. SANGSTER.

WHAT matter how the winds may blow,
Or blow they east, or blow they west ?
What reck I how the tides may flow,
Since ebb or flood alike is best ?

No summer calm, no winter gale,
  Impedes or drives me from my way;
I steadfast toward the haven sail
  That lies, perhaps, not far away.

What matter how the winds may blow?
  Since fair or foul alike is best;
God holds them in His hand, I know,
  And I may leave to Him the rest,
Assured that neither calm nor gale
  Can bring me danger or delay,
As still I toward the haven sail
  That lies, I know, not far away.

A. D. F. Randoiph.

I WAS sitting alone in the twilight,
  With spirit troubled and vexed,
With thoughts that were morbid and gloomy,
  And faith that was sadly perplexed.

Some homely work I was doing
  For the child of my love and care,
Some stitches half-wearily setting
  In the endless need of repair.

But my thoughts were about the " building,"
  The work some day to be tried,
And that only the gold and silver
  And the precious stone would abide :

And remembering my own poor efforts,
  The wretched work I had done,
And, even when trying most truly,
  The meager success I had won :

" It is nothing but wood, hay and stubble,"
  I said : " It will all be burned—
These useless fruits of the talents
  One day to be returned :

" And I have so longed to serve Him,
  And sometimes I know I have tried ;
But I'm sure when He sees such building
  He will never let it abide."

Just then as I turned the garment,
  That no rents should be left behind,
My eyes caught an odd little bungle
  Of mending and patchwork combined.

My heart grew suddenly tender,
  And something blinded my eyes,
With one of those sweet intuitions
  That sometimes make us so wise.

Dear child, she wanted to help me ;
I knew 'twas the best she could do ;
But oh, what a blotch she has made it—
The gray mis-matching the blue !

And yet—you can understand it ?—
With a tender smile and a tear,
And a half-compassionate yearning
I felt she had grown more dear.

Then a sweet voice broke the silence,
And the dear Lord said to me,
" Art thou tenderer for the little child
Than I am tender for thee ? "

Then straightway I knew His meaning,
So full of compassion and love,
And my faith came back to its refuge
Like the glad returning dove.

For I thought, when the Master-builder
Came down His temple to view,
To see what rents must be mended,
And what must be builded anew.

Perhaps, as He looks over the building,
He will bring my work to the light,
And seeing the marring and bungling,
And how far it all is from right,

He will feel as I felt for my darling,
   And will say as I said for her,
" Dear child, she wanted to help me,
   And love for me was the spur.

" And for the true love that's in it,
   The work shall seem perfect as mine,
And because it is willing service
   I will crown it with plaudits divine."

So there in the deepening twilight
   I seemed to be clasping a hand,
And to feel a great love constraining me
   Stronger than any command.

And I knew by the thrill of sweetness
   'Twas the hand of the Blessed One,
Which would tenderly guide and hold me
   Till all the labor is done.

So my thoughts are never more gloomy,
   My faith no longer is dim ;
But my heart is sunny and restful,
   And my eyes turned ever to Him.

                                   MRS. HERRICK JOHNSON.

HEIMGANG ! So the German people
Whisper, when they hear the bell
Tolling from some gray old steeple
  Death's familiar tale to tell ;
When they hear the organ dirges
  Swelling out from chapel dome,
And the singers' chanting surges,
  " Heimgang ! " always going home.

Heimgang ! Quaint and tender saying,
  In the grand old German tongue,
That hath shaped Melancthon's praying,
  And the hymns that Luther sung :
Blessèd is our loving Maker,
  That where'er our feet shall roam,
Still we journey towards " God's Acre "—
  Heimgang ! always going home.

———

ONE day at a time ! Every heart that aches
  Knows only too well how long that can seem ;
But it's never to-day that the spirit breaks,
  It's the darkened future without a gleam.

One day at a time ! 'Tis the whole of life !
  All sorrow, all joy are measured therein,
The bound of our purpose, our noblest strife
  The one only countersign, sure to win.

                    HELEN JACKSON (H. H.).

WE shall not die until our work be done ;
We shall not cease until our course be run :
We shall not fade or fail
While heart and faith prevail,
Or aught is to be won
Beneath the constant sun.

THE hands are such dear hands !
They are so full ; they turn at our demands
So often ; they reach out
With trifles scarcely thought about
So many times ; they do
So many things for me, for you—
If their fond wills mistake,
We may well bend, not break.

They are such fond, frail lips
That speak to us ! Pray if love strips
Them of discretion many times,
Or if they speak too slow, or quick, such crimes
We may pass by, for we may see
Days not far off when those small words may be
Held not as slow or quick or out of place, but dear,
Because the lips are no more here.

They are such dear familiar feet that go
Along the path with ours—feet fast or slow,
And trying to keep pace. If they mistake
Or tread upon some flower that we would take

Upon our breast, or bruise some reed,
Or crush poor Hope until it bleed,
We may be mute,
Nor turning quickly to impute
Grave fault ; for they and we
Have such a little way to go—can be
Together such a little while along the way,
We will be patient while we may.

So many little faults we find !
We see them, for not blind
To love.   We see them, but if you and I
Perhaps remember them some by-and-by
They will not be
Faults then—grave faults—to you and me,
But just odd ways, mistakes, or even less,
Remembrances to bless.
Days change so many things—yes, hours ;
We see so differently in sun and showers.
Mistaken words to-night
May be so cherished by to-morrow's light.
We may be patient, for we know
There's such a little way to go.
N. Y. Independent.

" I'll drop my burden at His feet
And bear a song away ! "

OVER the narrow foot-path
That led from my lowly door,
I went with a thought of the Master,
As oft I had walked before.

My heart was heavily laden,
 And with tears my eyes were dim ;
But I knew I should lose the burden
 Could I get a glimpse of Him.

It was more than I could carry,
 If I carried it all alone ;
And none in my house might share it—
 Only One on the throne.
It came between me and pleasure,
 Between my work and me ;
But our Lord could understand it,
 And His touch could set me free.

Over the trodden pathway,
 To the fields all shorn and bare,
I went with a step that faltered,
 And a face that told of care.
I had lost the light of the morning,
 With its shimmer of sun and dew ;
But a gracious look of the Master
 Would the strength of morn renew.

While yet my courage wavered,
 And the sky before me blurred,
I heard a voice behind me
 Saying a tender word.
And I turned to see the brightness
 Of Heaven upon the road,

And sudden I lost the pressure
Of the weary, crushing load.

Nothing that hour was altered,
I had still the weight of care ;
But I bore it now with the gladness
Which comes of answered prayer.
Not a grief the soul can fetter
Nor cloud its vision, when
The dear Lord gives the spirit
To breathe to his will, amen.

O friends ! if the greater burdens
His love can make so light,
Why should His wonderful goodness
Our halting credence slight ?
The little sharp vexations,
And the briars that catch and fret,
Shall we not take them to the Helper
Who has never failed us yet ?

Tell Him about the heartache,
And tell Him the longings, too ;
Tell Him the baffled purpose,
When we scarce know what to do.
Then, leaving all our weakness
With the One divinely strong,
Forget that we bore the burden,
And carry away the song.

MARGARET E. SANGSTER.

WHAT, tears in your eyes, my beloved !
Memories of trouble and loss !
Can you not thank Him for the anguish ?
Can you not bless Him for the cross ?
He knows and loves. Unnoted of Him
Not one of these tears shall fall.
Look up through their shining, dear heart and say,
I bless thee, O Master, for all !

MABEL.

THE cup of my years was filling—
It had almost reached the brim—
As I sat by my lonely fireside
Singing a Sabbath hymn.
I was sick and alone and weary,
And I sought in vain for rest,
And I longed for the tender sympathy
With which I once was blest.

I sat alone by my fireside,
And for very weakness wept,
And my tears kept mingling with my song
Until, at last, I slept.
I slept, and I thought in my sleeping
I was mounting a giddy height,
A heavy burden was in my arms,
And it was almost night.

I was weary and weak and trembling,
   And hardly a step could take,
Hardly a whisper could I speak
   Or upward progress make.
"Oh, for a friend," I faltered ;
   And even as I cried,
A step was coming down the height,
   A form was by my side.

A face was gazing into mine,
   With tender, pitying eyes ;
An arm was underneath my own,
   And helping me to rise.
Up, through the rocky pathway,
   Up, towards the distant blue,
We went ; I gazed into the face,
   And it seemed like one I knew.

And oh, the tender sympathy,
   That cannot be expressed,
Through all my being seemed to flow
   And filled it full of rest.
My burden seemed as nothing,
   And, though no word he spoke,
I knew that Jesus Christ was there ;
   "Dear Lord !" I said, and woke.

The cup of my years is brimming,
   And I gladly see it fill,
And I sit by myself, but not alone,
   For Christ is with me still.

Weak, and yet full of resting,
  I have no vain alarms,
For underneath me now I feel
  The everlasting arms.

J. H. M.

WHEN sorrow's darkest night
Above, around, like a thick cloud doth fall,
  Though thou canst see no light,
Yet God still lives, and watches over all.

  Then trust His loving care ;
Pray always, though thy feeble sight be dim ;
  Thy burdens He will bear,
If thou canst only leave all things with Him.

JULIA D. PECK.

THE night is come ; like to the day,
  Depart not Thou, great God, away.
Let not my sins, black as the night,
Eclipse the luster of Thy light:
Keep in my horizon : for to me
The sun makes not the day, but Thee.
Thou, whose nature cannot sleep,
On my temples sentry keep :

Guard me against those watchful foes
Whose eyes are open while mine close.
Let no dreams my head infest,
But such as Jacob's temple blest.
While I do rest, my soul advance ;
Make my sleep a holy trance :
That I may, my rest being wrought,
Awake into some holy thought,
And with as active vigor run
My course as doth the nimble sun.
Sleep is a death : Oh, make me try
By sleeping, what it is to die ;
And as gently lay my head
On my grave as on my bed.

Sir Thomas Browne, 1605.

I SAID, one day, "O'life ! you're little worth.
Made up of toil and care and blighted hope,
With pain and sin and all their ills to cope,
The day of death is better than of birth."
Ev'en as I spoke, Love put a hand in mine,
And its dear presence drove all gloom away,
As shadows flee before the dawn of day,
And life became a heritage divine !

Laura Garland Carr.

WE shall be like Him "—strange the story !
Will wonders never cease ?
We shall be like the King of Glory !
Like Him, the Prince of Peace !

It must be true ! for carefully
I've read this passage o'er ;
It plainly says that we shall be
Like Him whom I adore.

O, tell me, does it really mean
'Tis possible on earth
To be all glorious within,
Like Him of lowly birth ?

Or does it mean that we must wait
To lay this earth-robe by ?
I grow impatient with the thought
And long to mount the sky.

I'll read it o'er again.   It says
That when He doth appear
We shall be like Him ; it must mean
We shall be like Him here !

For, oh, last night, while bowing low
Before my Father's throne,
I saw His face, and oh ! I felt
His strong hand clasp my own.

You smile, and tell me 'tis by faith
  And not by sight I see :
If such the fact, makes it the sight
  A whit less real to me ?

Wouldst have me think that faith is but
  Some *ignis fatuus* light
No, no, 'tis all the same to me
  Whether 'tis faith or sight.

And this I know, for 'twas His voice
  Which spoke thus in my ear :
" If we would dwell with Him above
  We must be like him here ! "

                    HARRIET CHASE.

W E need not *die* to go to God !
    See, how the daily prayer is given,—
'Tis not across a gulf we cry
  " Our Father who dost dwell in heaven ! "

And, " Let Thy will on earth be done,
  As in Thy heaven," by this thy child !
What is it but all prayers in one,
  That soul and sense be reconciled ?

A S the poor panting hart to the water-brook runs
   As the water-brook runs to the sea,
So earth's fainting daughters and famishing sons
   O Fountain of love, run to Thee !

ALICE CARY.

A CROSS the hedges, thick with autumn flowers,
   I watch the wild, rough wind's breath come and
      go,
Bending the leaves until their pale backs show ;
And each small bird that there for safety cowers,
To hide before the storm that darkly lowers
Is shown to us, who did not even know
They shivered there—for they were hidden so—
Until the wind put forth its strongest powers.
Is not this like some life of sweetest rest—
Passing its years in a most even course
Through sun and summer's perfect, peaceful smile ?
Yet, when rough trials search that quiet breast,
It shows beneath the calm, that love's vast force
Has lain there, hiding humbly, all the while.

F ORGIVE ! that oft my spirit wears
   Her time and strength in trivial cares;
Enfold her in Thy changeless peace,
So she from all but Thee may cease !

ANGELUS SILESIUS, 1657.

THE coiled elastic spring of steel
   Imprisoned in its brazen bars,
Moving each ruby-balanced wheel,
   Measures its motion with the stars.

The heart's low pulse, the firmer beat,
   The throbbing of the burdened brain,
The music of a million feet
   On hill-top and on grassy plain;

The sea's majestic ebb and flow,
   The ripple on the tender rill,
The gentle falling of the snow,
   The bird-note and the viol's trill;

With these, and in the march of thought
   Mid passions ripened into wars,
Mid the many things which time has wrought,
   Our life is stepping with the stars.

It is not peace that reigns alone
   In those stupendous orbs of fire,
But rent and scarred from zone to zone,
   They melt and crumble and expire.

Yet discord is but harmony
   Which mortals do not understand,
The tear, the laughter and the sigh,
   Touch in one note the immortal strand.

We rotate in our little cell,
And touch each other through the bars.
But God has ordered all things well
Who keeps us stepping with the stars.

E. E. ADAMS.

A CROSS the field of daily work
   Run the footpaths leading—where ?
Run they east or run they west,
   One way all the workers fare :
Every awful thing of earth,
   Sin and pain and battle-noise,
Every dear thing—baby's birth,
   Faces, flowers, or lovers' joys—
     Is a wicket gate where we
     Join the great highway to Thee !

Restless, restless, speed we on ;
   Whither in the vast unknown ?
Not to you and not to me
   Are the sealèd orders shown ;
But the Hand that built the road,
   And the Light that leads the feet,
And this inward restlessness,
   Are such invitation sweet,
     That where I no longer see
     Highway still must lead to Thee.

WILLIAM C. GANNETT.

LORD, according to Thy words,
  I *have* considered Thy birds ;
And find their life good,
And better, the better understood;
Sowing neither corn nor wheat,
They have all that they can eat;
Reaping no more than they sow,
They have all that they can stow ;
Having neither barn nor store,
Hungry again they eat more.

Considering, I see too that they
Have a busy life and plenty of play ;
In the earth they dig their bills deep,
And work well, though they do not reap;
Then to play in the air they are not loath,
And their nests between are better than both.
But this is when there blow no storms,
When berries are plenty in winter and worms;
When their feathers are thick and oil is enough
To keep the cold out,—and the rain off.
If there should come a long, hard frost,
Then it looks as Thy birds were lost.

But I considered further, and find
A hungry bird has a free mind ;
He is hungry to-day, not to-morrow ;
Steals no comfort, no grief doth borrow ;
This moment is his, Thy will hath said it,
The nest is nothing till Thou hast made it.

The bird has pain, but has no fear,
Which is the worst of any gear ;
When cold and hunger and harm betide him,
He gathers them not to stuff inside him :
Content with the day's ill he has got,
He just waits, nor haggles with his lot ;
Neither jumbles God's will
With dribblets from his own still.

But next I see in my endeavor,
The birds here do not live forever ;
That cold or hunger, sickness or age,
Finishes their earthly stage ;
The rook drops without a stroke,
And never gives another croak ;
Birds lie here, and birds lie there,
With little feathers all astare ;
And in Thy own sermon, Thou
That the sparrow falls, dost allow.

It shall not cause me any alarm ;
For neither so comes the bird to harm ;
Seeing our Father,—Thou hast said,
Is by the sparrow's dying bed !
Therefore, it is a blessèd place,
And the sparrow in high grace !
It cometh, therefore, to this, Lord ;
I have considered Thy word,
And henceforth will be Thy bird.

GEO. MACDONALD.

SOME day or other I shall surely come
    Where true hearts wait for me ;
Then let me learn the language of that home
    While here on earth I be,
Lest my poor lips for want of words be dumb
    In that High Company.

LOUISE CHANDLER MOULTON.

THE shady nooks and corners,
    So quiet and so cool,
Where springs the crystal streamlet,
    Where glooms the dusky pool—
I leave the path to seek them ;
    No dearer haunts I know
Than just the lonely places
    Where patient mosses grow.

The shady nooks and corners
    By forest, brook and burn,
They hide in deep recesses
    The waving feathery fern.
And through their sheltered silence
    Shy wings flit to and fro,
And bits of song are breaking
    Where humble flowers blow.

The shady nooks and corners
  Apart from stir and strife,
And distant from the tumult
  Of busy whirling life,
Where some of God's dear children
  Alone are left and low,
There, star-like, strong and steadfast,
  The lights of promise glow.

The shady nooks and corners,
  Wherein we dwell with God,
And conquer pain and weakness,
  Sustained by staff and rod ;
Perhaps in all earth's journey
  Naught sweeter shall we know
Than just these sanctuaries
  Where hidden graces grow.

The shady nooks and corners
  Screened from the glaring day :—
Songs in the night He giveth
  To those who watch and pray,
And blessing comes when leaving
  The trodden road we go
To rest amid the shadows
  Where living waters flow.

                          MARGARET E. SANGSTER.

OH, the temple of the soul ; of what tiny stones
'tis built !
A simple prayer for one whose life may have been
stained with guilt :—
The drying of an infant's tear, a smile to cheer some
heart,
A word to soften envy's shaft, or turn away its dart.

All trifles, yet our pitying Lord in mercy takes the
whole,
And fashions from them in His love, a temple for
the soul ;
Cements the fragments—asking naught beyond our
power to give—
Leading us, step by step, to see how grand it is to
live.—

To live to do some noble work, howe'er obscure it
be !
To live to pluck away the thorns that grow upon
life's tree,
To scatter smiles and helpful words, although the
way be rough,
To smooth life's path for tender feet, is this not joy
enough ?

Oh, the temple of the soul ! it is very sweet to know,
If we fully trust our Father's care, whatever fierce
winds blow,

Though life's billows may dash o'er us, and its surges
    fiercely roll,
They ne'er can touch the inner life, the temple of the
    soul.

E VER and ever the world goes round,
    Bearing its burdens and crosses ;
Ever and ever the years roll on,
    With their tide of sorrows and losses.
Ever and ever the book of life
    Bears upon its pages
The weary, weary lay of the heart,
    Sung through all the ages.

Ever and ever with outstretched hands
    We grasp for a golden morrow ;
Ever and ever the billows of time
    Are freighted with bitter sorrow ;
Ever and ever the lips smile on,
    That the world may walk in blindness ;
Little they know of the heart's wild woe,
    When the face looks but with brightness.

Ever and ever the shadows fall,
    Over the golden mosses ;
Ever a gleam from Paradise,
    Lightens our cares and crosses.

Ever and ever the morning dawns
  On hopes that are breathed in gladness;
Ever and ever the night brings in
  Its tide of bitter sadness.
Ever and ever the eye of God
  Looketh upon us with pity,
And ever the light is shown to us,
  That gleams from the Golden City.

HAVING won by toil and pain ,
  Who shall regret the pangs of life ?
Who would regret the Past's long night,
With all its fear and chill and blight,
If now the east, through twilight gray,
Were streaked with Everlasting Day ?

I WALK down the Valley of Silence,
  Down the dim, voiceless valley alone ;
And I hear not the fall of a footstep
  Around me—save God's and my own ;
And the hush of my heart is as holy
  As hovers when angels have flown.

Long ago I was weary of voices
   Whose music my heart could not win;
Long ago I was weary of noises
   That fretted my soul with their din;
Long ago I was weary of places
   Where I met but the human and sin.

I walked through the world with the worldly;
   I craved what the world never gave ;
And I said, " In the world each ideal
   That shines like a star on life's wave,
Is tossed on the shores of the Real,
   And sleeps like a dream in the grave."

And still did I pine for the perfect,
   And still found the false with the true ;
I sought 'mid the human for heaven,
   But caught a mere glimpse of the blue,
And I wept when the clouds of the mortal,
   Veiled even that glimpse from my view.

And I toiled on, heart-tired of human ;
   And I moaned 'mid the masses of men,
Till I knelt long at an altar,
   And heard a voice call me—since then
I walked down the Valley of Silence
   That is far beyond mortal ken.

Do you ask what I found in the Valley ?
   'Tis my trysting place with the Divine;
And I fell at the feet of the Holy,
   And above me a voice said, " Be mine."

And there rose from the depths of my spirit
The echo, " My heart shall be thine."

Do you ask how I live in the Valley ?
I weep and I dream and I pray ;
But my tears are as sweet as the dew-drops
That fall on the roses in May :
And my prayers, like a perfume from censers,
Ascending to God night and day.

In the hush of the Valley of Silence
I dream all the songs that I sing.
And the music floats down the dim valley
Till each finds a word for a wing,
That to men, like the dove of the deluge,
The message of peace they may bring.

But far on the deep there are billows
That never shall break on the beach,
And I have heard songs in the silence
That never shall float into speech ;
And I have dreams in the Valley
Too lofty for language to reach.

Do you ask me the place in the Valley,
Ye hearts that are narrowed by care ?
It lies far away between mountains,
And God and His angels are there ;
And one is the dark Mount of Sorrow,
And one the bright Mountain of Prayer.

FATHER RYAN.

ALL common things, each day's events,
   That with the hour begin and end,
Our pleasures and our discontents,
   Are rounds by which we may ascend.

LONGFELLOW.

THE way is long, my darling,
   The road is rough and steep,
And fast across the evening sky
   I see the shadows sweep.
But oh, my love, my darling,
   No ill to us can come,
No terror turn us from the path,
   For we are going home.

Your feet are tired, my darling—
   So tired, the tender feet ;
But think, when we are there at last,   .
   How sweet the rest ! how sweet !
For lo ! the lamps are lighted,
   And yonder gleaming dome,
Before us, shining like a star,
   Shall guide our footsteps home.

Art cold, my love, and famished ?
   Art faint and sore athirst ?
Be patient yet a little while,
   And joyous, as at first ;

For oh ! the sun sets never
Within that land of bloom,
And thou shalt eat the bread of life
And drink life's wine at home.

The wind blows cold, my darling,
Adown the mountain steep,
And thick across the evening sky
The darkling shadows creep ;
But oh ! my love, press onward,
Whatever trials come,
For in the way the Father set,
We two are going home.

MARGARET E. SANGSTER.

. . . WHY forecast the trials of life,
With such sad and grave persistence,
And wait and watch for a crowd of ills
That as yet have no existence ?

Strength for to-day—what a precious boon
For earnest souls who labor !
For the willing hands who minister
To the needy friend or neighbor.

Strength for to-day that the weary hearts
In the battle for right may quail not ;
And the eyes bedimmed by bitter tears
In the search for light may fail not.

Strength for to-day on the downhill track
  For the travelers near the valley;
That up, far up on the other side
  Ere long they may safely rally.

Strength for to-day, that our precious youth
  May happily shun temptation,
And build from the rise to the set of the sun
  On a strong and sure foundation.

Strength for to-day, in house and home
  To practice forbearance sweetly;
To scatter kind words and loving deeds,
  Still trusting in God completely.

Strength for to-day is all that we need,
  For there never will be a to-morrow;
For to-morrow will prove but another to-day,
  With its measures of joy and sorrow.

I F you sit down at set of sun
  And count the acts that you have done,
    And counting find
One self-denying act—one word
That eased the heart of him who heard,
    One glance most kind,
That fell like sunshine where it went,
Then you may count the day well spent.

"THE days are all alike," she said ;
   " The glory of my life is dead ;
Hope and ambition far are fled—
   And I live on in vain.

"Others have reached the leaves of fame,
Others have won undying name ;
My shadowed hours are still the same—
   What comfort doth remain ?

To clothe—to feed—to satisfy
The household need ; the children's cry
Doth fill the moments as they fly ;
   My sheaves are poor and small.

"So full the claims of every day
I scarce can creep to Thee, and pray ;
Oh, lead me in some brighter way
   To glorify Thy name."

Then spoke the Master, "Thankful be,
My child ! that God hath honored thee,
The richest crown of life to see,
   That prayers and hopes can claim.

"Glory thou cravedst—and instead
I gave thee children to be fed,
Those tender lives that look for bread
   Unto the mo her hand.

"Joy didst thou seek—I heard thy prayer;
I sent thee infant faces fair,
And rosy lips and sunny hair—
    A blessèd, sinless band."

"'Glory to God,' was still my plea—
Patience of Christ they brought from Me—
These babes that God shall ask of thee,
    Within the resting land."

                                    ?

THERE'S many a rest on the road of life,
    If we only would stop to take it,
And many a tone from the better land,
    If the careworn heart would wake it.
To the sunny soul that is full of hope,
    And whose beautiful trust ne'er faileth,
The grass is green and the flowers are bright,
    Though the wintry storm prevaileth.

Better to hope, though the clouds hang low,
    And to keep the eyes still lifted;
For the sweet blue sky will soon peep through
    When the ominous clouds are rifted.
There was never a night without a day,
    Nor an evening without a morning;
And the darkest hour, the proverb goes,
    Is the hour before the dawning.

Better to weave in the web of life
A bright and golden filling,
And to do God's will with a ready heart,
And hands that are swift and willing,
Than to snap the delicate silver threads
Of our curious lives asunder,
And then blame Heaven for the tangled ends,
And sit to grieve and wonder.

THE faint low echo that we hear of far-off music
seems to fill
The silent air with love and fear, and the world's
clamors all grow still,
Until the portals close again, and leave us toiling on
in pain.

Complain not that the way is long,—what road is
weary that leads there ?
But let the Angel take thy hand, and lead thee up
the misty stair,
Andthen with beating heart await the opening of
the Golden Gate.

ADELAIDE ANNE PROCTOR.

HOW many of us have ships at sea,
Freighted with wishes, hopes and fears,
Tossing about on the waves, while we
Linger and wait on the shore for years,

Gazing afar through the distance dim
And sighing, " Will ever our ships come in ? "

We sent them away with laughter and song,
   The decks were white and the sails were new,
The fragrant breezes bore them along,
   The sea was calm and the skies were blue,
And we thought as we watched them sail away
Of the joy they would bring us some future day.

Long have we watched beside the shore
   To catch the gleam of a coming sail,
But we only hear the breakers' roar,
   Or the sweeping night-wind's dismal wail,
Till our cheeks grow pale, and our eyes grow dim,
And we sadly sigh, " Will they never come in ? "

Oh ! poor sad heart with its burden of cares,
   Its aims defeated, its worthless life,
That has garnered only the thorns and the tares
   That is seared and torn in the pitiful strife.
Afar on the heavenly golden shore
Thy ships are anchored forevermore.

FLORENCE GROVER.

ONE of these days it will all be over,
   Sorrow and parting, and loss and gain,
Meetings and partings of friends and lover,
   Joy that was ever so edged with pain.

One of these days will our hands be folded,
One of these days will the work be done,
Finishèd the pattern our lives have molded,
Ended our labor beneath the sun.

One of these days will the heart-ache leave us,
One of these days will the burden drop ;
Never again shall a hope deceive us,
Never again will our progress stop.
Freed from the blight of vain endéavor,
Winged with the health of immortal life,
One of these days we shall quit forever
All that is vexing in earthly strife.

One of these days we shall know the reason,
Haply, of much that perplexes now ;
One of these days in the Lord's good season
Light of his peace shall adorn the brow.
Blest, though out of tribulation,
Lifted to dwell in his sun-bright smile,
Happy to share in the great salvation,
Well may we tarry a little while.

.   .   .   SHALL we sit idly down and say
The night hath come ; it is no longer day ?
The night hath *not* yet come ; we are not quite
Cut off from labor by the failing light ;

Something remains for us to do or dare ;
Even the oldest tree some fruit may bear ;
   .   .   .   .   .   .
For age is opportunity no less
Than youth itself, though in another dress,
And as the evening   .   .   .   fades away,
The sky is filled with stars, invisible by day.

        From LONGFELLOW'S " MORITURI SALUTAMUS."

THANKS for the benediction of Thy love
   Celestial, falling with a heavenly grace
From out those heights where angel ones, above
   The scenes of our temptations, gladly trace
The paths by which our feet may safely climb
Those starry heights beyond, where life shall grow
   sublime.

               HESTER M. POOLE.

IX.

SONGS OF REMEMBRANCE.

" I will remember Thee, in the night-watches."

" The dawn is not distant,
Nor is the night starless ;
Love is eternal !
God is still God, and
His faith shall not fail us ! "

" Here then inscribe them—each red-letter day !
Forget not all the sunshine of the way
By which the Lord hath led thee ! answered prayers,
And joys unasked ; strange blessings, lifted cares,—
Grand promise echoes ! Thus each page shall be
A record of God's faithfulness to thee."

SONS OF REMEMBRANCE.

" O Life and Love ! O happy throng
Of thoughts, whose only speech is song."

H IDE thee awhile, call back the troublous past;
How many times we have been wakened thus,
while I,
Entered the dreadful shadow, all aghast,
And found beyond it a far brighter sky ;
How oft the low black clouds above me lay,
And some sweet wind of God blew them away.

Hide thee awhile, call back the happy past :
Thy many marvelous mercies: thy delicious days,
When sorrow watched thee from afar, nor cast
One shadow o'er love's many changing ways ;
All eyes have wept ; life no new sorrow has ;
Times come and go ; but God is where He was.

So, soul, come with me, and be sure we'll find
  A little sanctuary, wherein dwell faith and prayer,
Then, if misfortune come, cast doubt behind ;
  We shall have strength to fight, or strength to
      bear ;
No prisoners of evil fate are we,
For in our breast we carry Hopeful's key.

AMELIA E. BARR.

S UM up at night what thou hast done by day;
  And in the morning what thou hast to do.
Dress and undress thy soul.

GEORGE HERBERT.

T HE things o'er which we grieved, with lashes
    wet,
Will flash before us out of life's dark night,
As stars shine most in deeper tints of blue.

THEY are poor
That have lost nothing : they are poorer far
Who, losing, have forgotten ; they most poor
Of all, who lose and wish they might forget.

For life is one, and in its warp and woof
There runs a thread of gold that glitters fair,
And sometimes in the pattern shows most sweet
Where there are somber colors.   It is true
That we have wept.   But oh ! this thread of gold,
We would not have it tarnish ; let us turn
Oft and look back upon the wondrous web,
And when it shineth, sometimes we shall know
That memory is possession.

When I remember something which I had,
   But which is gone, and I must do without,
I sometimes wonder how I can be glad ;
   Even in cowslip time, when hedges sprout,
It makes me sigh to think on it,—but yet
My days will not be better days, should I forget.

When I remember something promised me,
   But which I never had, nor can have now,
Because the promiser we no more see
   In countries that accord with mortal vow ;—
When I remember this, I mourn—but yet
My happier days are not the days when I forget.

JEAN INGELOW.

FROM the mountain-side of years,
   Up which I came and failed or won,
The places watered by my tears
   Seem sweet as gardens in the sun.

From this calm height my way seems plain,
    And work and duty shall be joy,
Ripened, toned down, and purged by pain
    No ill my purpose can destroy.

To-day, I seem to understand
    That pain and struggle, grief and care,
Are chisels in an Unseen Hand,
    That round us into statues fair.

A. P. MILLER.

SUMMER days
And moonlight nights, He led us over paths
Bordered with pleasant flowers ; but when His steps
Were on the mighty waters,—when we went
With trembling hearts through nights of pain and
    loss,—
His smile was sweeter and His love more dear;
And only Heaven is better, than to walk
With Christ at midnight, over moonless seas !

" B. M."

IN dreams that hold
One hand to forward, one to past
We stay the years that fly so fast,
    And link our new lives to the old.

F. W. BOURDILLON.

THINK ye the notes of holy song
  On Milton's tuneful ear have died ?
Think ye that Raphael's angel throng
  Have vanished from his side ?

Oh, no ! we live our life again ;
  Or warmly touched, or coldly dim,
The pictures of the past remain,—
  Man's work shall follow him.

                       WHITTIER.

THERE was a time when meadow, grove and
      stream,
The earth and every common sight,
      To me did seem
    Appareled in celestial light,—
The glory and the freshness of a dream.
It is not now as it hath been of yore :
    Turn wheresoe'er I may,
    By night or day,
The things which I have seen I now can see no more.

    The rainbow comes and goes
    And lovely is the rose ;
    The moon doth with delight
Look 'round her when the heavens are bare ;
    Waters on a starry night
    Are beautiful and fair ;

The sunshine is a glorious birth ;
But yet I know, where'er I go,
That there hath passed away a glory from the earth.

O joy ! that in our embers
Is something that doth live,
That nature yet remembers
What was so fugitive !
The thought of our past years in me doth breed
Perpetual benediction :   .   .   .

.   .   .   .

Though inland far we be,
Our souls have sight of that immortal sea
Which brought us hither,—
Can in a moment travel thither,
And see the children sport upon the shore,
And hear the mighty waters rolling evermore.

Then sing, sing a joyous song !

.   .   .   .

Though nothing can bring back the hour
Of splendor in the grass, of glory in the flower,—
We will grieve not, rather find
Strength in what remains behind ;
In the primal sympathy
Which having been, must ever be ;
In the soothing thoughts that spring
Out of human suffering ;
In the faith that looks through death,
In years that bring the philosophic mind.

WORDSWORTH.

I MIND the weary days of old,
   When motionless I seemed to lie ;
The nights when fierce the billows rolled,
   And changed my course, I knew not why.
I feared the calm, I feared the gale,
   Foreboding danger and delay,
Forgetting I was thus to sail
   To reach what seemed so far away.

I measure not the loss and fret
   Which through those years of doubt I bore ;
I keep the memory fresh, and yet
   Would hold God's patient mercy more.
What wrecks have passed me in the gale,
   What ships gone down on summer days ;
While I, with furled or spreading sail,
   Stood for the haven far away.

                              A. D. F. RANDOLPH.

 .   .   .   .

THERE is no soul but has some deep regret
   For something lost on which the heart was set ;
Through tear-drop prisms still we see it glow,
Rimmed with the splendors of the glorious bow.
There is no soul but sometimes takes its flight
To those far skies that made its youth so bright,
In search of something lost, and with a sigh,
Gives o'er the search, returns and waits to die,
And treads the stony way with bleeding feet,
To find it when the heart has ceased to beat.

 .   .   .   .

O sweet autumnal days of long ago !
How in my bosom yet their raptures glow !
Those mellow days, when in the infinite West,
In some celestial islands of the blest,
The angels loosed the winds and set them free,
To roam the fields and woods and hills with me,
While toiling men in hamlets far away
Heard the woods roar through all the balmy day.
O blessèd days of sunshine and of peace !
When from the strife of man I stole release
And walked abroad among the hills and woods
In the sweet company of God's solitudes ;
Through velvet fields I saw the rivers run
And white towns shining in the mellow sun,
And heard the woods their soothing music pour
From forest harps with multitudinous roar,
Or saw across some blue and distant bay
A glory fall on cities far away,
And taper steeples, tow'ring slim and high,
Stand glorified against the wondrous sky !
And then God came with His rich gifts of power
And talked and walked with me from hour to hour,
And changed me to a harp of living chords.

.   .   .   .

"Consolation," A. P. Miller.

THE sudden joys that out of darkness start
As flames from ashes ; swift desires that dart
Like swallows singing down each wind that blows !
White as the gleam of a receding sail,

White as a cloud that floats and fades in air,
White as the whitest lily on a stream,
These tender memories are : a fairy tale
Of some enchanted land, we know not where,
But lovely as a landscape in a dream !

LONGFELLOW.

THE happy dreams that gladdened all our youth
When dreams had less of self and more of truth;
The childhood's faith, so tranquil and so sweet,
Which sat like Mary at the Master's feet—
These are not lost.

Not lost, O Lord ! for in thy city bright,
Our eyes shall see the past by clearer light,
And things long hidden from our gaze below,
Thou wilt reveal, and we shall surely know—
These are not lost.

O MEMORY, ope thy mystic door ;
O dream of youth return ;
And let the light that gleamed of yore
Beside this altar burn.

The past is plain ; 'twas love designed
E'en sorrow's iron chain ;
And mercy's shining thread has twined
With the dark warp of pain.

DAVID GRAY.

. . . . . . No strain
That e'er awakened human smiles or tears
Is lost ; nor shall we call it back in vain.
Beside the shore, amid the eternal spheres,
Hark, the belovèd voices once again
Rise from the winds and waves to soothe mine ears.

SOME comfort when all else is night,
About his fortune plays,
Who sets his dark to-days in the light
Of the sunnier yesterdays.

. . . .

In memory of joy that's been
Something of joy, is still ;
Where no dew is, we may dabble in
A *dream* of the dew at will.

. . . .

Thank God, when other power decays,
And other pleasures die,
We still may set our dark to-days,
In the light of days gone by.

ALICE CARY.

NOT to forget, when pain and grief draw nigh,
Into the ocean of time past, to dive
For memories of God's mercies.

HENRY SEPTIMUS SUTTON.

WHEN doomed to feel that youth is o'er,
That spring and summer both have fled,
That we can wake to life no more,
The buds and blossoms that are dead ;
That evermore the years will steal
Some brightness as they hurry on,
And with the past we know and feel
The glory of our life is gone ;

And still, the skies are just as blue,
The golden suns as warm and bright,
No star has lost its radiant hue,
Or faded from the crown of night ;
And beauty's cheek is still as fair,
The songs of birds as sweet at morn,
The flowers bloom, and in the air
The fragrance of the spring is born.

But oh, to think of all the past,
How much of good there was to glean,
How little came to us at last,
And yet, and yet, what might have been !
How shadows gather o'er the heart,
The night winds bear a sadder strain ;
The eyes grow dim with tears that start,
And memory's gates we close in vain.

B UILD thee more stately mansions, O my soul,
As the swift seasons roll !
Leave thy low-vaulted past !
Let each new temple, nobler than the last,
Shut thee from heaven with a dome more vast,
Till thou at length art free,
Leaving thine outgrown shell by life's unresting sea !

OLIVER WENDELL HOLMES.

X.

SONGS IN SICKNESS.

" The mark of rank in Nature
    Is capacity for pain,
And the anguish of the singer
    Makes the sweetness of the strain ! '

" There's a purpose in pain,
    Else it were devilish ! "

" If broken lives may best complete
    Thy circle, let our fragments fall
        An offering at Thy feet."

SONGS IN SICKNESS.

God has use for all thy pain.

I TRUST in my soul
That the great master hand which sweeps over the
 whole
Of this deep harp of life, if at moments it stretch
To shrill tension some one wailing nerve, means to
 fetch
Its response the truest, most stringent and smart,—
Its pathos the purest, from out the wrung heart,
Whose faculties, flaccid it may be, if less
Sharply strung, sharply smitten, had failed to ex-
 press
Just the one note, the great harmony needs.

OWEN MERIDITH's "*Lucille.*"

THIS leaf? this stone? It is thy heart;
 It must be crushed by pain and smart,
It must be cleansed by sorrow's art—

Ere it will yield a fragrance sweet,
Ere it will shine a jewel meet,
To lay before thy dear Lord's feet.

THE same old baffling questions ! O my friend
I cannot answer them. In vain I send
My soul into the dark, where never burn
The lamps of science, nor the natural light
Of Reason's sun and stars ! I cannot learn
Their great and solemn meanings, nor discern
The awful secrets of the eyes which turn
Evermore on us through the day and night,
With silent challenge, and a dumb demand,
Proffering the riddles of the dread unknown
Like the calm sphinxes with their eyes of stone,
Questioning the centuries from their veils of sand.
I have no answer for myself or thee,
Save that I learned at my mother's knee :
  " All is of God that is, and is to be,
And God is good ! " Let this suffice us still
Resting in child-like trust upon His will,
Who moveth His great ends unthwarted by the ill.

                                        WHITTIER.

I KNOW Thy wondrous ways will end
In love and blessing, Thou true friend!

Enough if Thou art ever near.
I know whom Thou wilt glorify
And raise o'er sun and stars on high,
  Thou lead'st through depths of darkness here

                    I WAIT,
Till from my veiled brows shall fall
        This being's thrall,
Which keeps me now from knowing all.
In stormless mornings yet to be
I'll pluck from Life's full fruited tree,
    The joys to-day denied to me.

MARY CLEMMER.

THEY who have learned to pray aright,
    From Pain's dark well draw up delight.

THE Border-Lands are calm and still,
    And solemn are their silent shades ;
And my heart welcomes them, until
    The light of life's long evening fades.

I heard them spoken of with dread,
    As fearful and unquiet places ;
Shades where the living and the dead
    Looked sadly in each other's faces.

But since Thy hand hath led me here
And I have seen the Border-Land—
Seen the dark river flowing near,
  Stood on its brink as now I stand,

There has been nothing to alarm
  My trembling soul ; how could I fear
While thus encircled with Thine arm ?
  I never felt Thee half so near.

They say the waves are dark and deep,
  That faith has perished in the river ;
They speak of death with fear, and weep,
  Shall my soul perish ? Never ! never !

I know that Thou wilt never leave
  The soul that trembles while it clings
To Thee : I know Thou wilt achieve
  Its passage on Thine outspread wings.

And since I first was brought so near
  The stream that flows to the Dead Sea,
I think that it has grown more clear
  And shallow than it used to be.

ONCE Pain beat upon my heart
  And well-nigh killed it.
I shuddered at the smart,
  But said " God willed it."

And down and down again,
  With awful power,
Fell the great hand of Pain,
  Hour after hour.

While like a mighty flail,
  The fierce blows hurt me,
I cried, " God doth prevail,
  He'll not desert me."

Blow upon cruel blow,
  The great hand gave me,
Yet I cried, " He doth know
  And He will save me."

I did not loudly cry,
  And ask God's reason ;
I knew He'd tell me why
  In His own season.

" In His good time," I said,
  In trusting blindness,
And I was not afraid
  To wait His kindness.

I did not trust in vain,
  God drew me nearer,
And whispered, " Smile again !
  The way is clearer."

And lo ! my mortal sight
Could reach to heaven,
My faith dispelled the night,
And light was given.

ELLA WHEELER.

I HAVE some songs I do not sing
To any human ear ;
None can discern the precious thing
Which is to me so dear.

No sympathy goes far enough ;
No soul comes into mine ;
No critic's voice but sounds too rough,
For me to lend a line.

They are my songs, my precious songs,
That come to me by night ;
Their very rhythmic pulse belongs
To fancy's farthest flight.

In them my spirit moved at will
Between the earth and sky ;
I cannot catch again the thrill
I felt when stars passed by.

So blame me not ; I cannot sing,
  To any human ear,
Those anthems of my suffering
  Which are to me so dear.

REV. SAMUEL DUFFIELD.

WHAT though the web our hands shall leave
      undone
Be tangled, and its pattern feebly wrought ?
If it be finished by some stronger one,
  The stronger soul may win the goal we sought.
    .   .   .   .
Some soul shall reap what we have sown in tears.

LAURA B. BOYCE.

IF I must win my way to perfectness
  In the sad path of suffering, like Him
The over-flowing river of whose life
Touches the flood-mark of humanity
On the white pillars of the heavenly throne,
Then welcome . . . . sickness . . .
Sorrow and pain, the fear and fact of death !

DR. J. G. HOLLAND.

.   .   .   .   .   .

WHAT profit to lay on God's altar
        Oblations of pain ?—

Can He in the infinite gladness
    That floods all His being with light
Complacently look on the sadness
    That dares to intrude on His sight ?
Can He, in His rhythmic creation
    Attuned to the chant of the spheres,
Bear the discord of moans, the vibration
    Of down-dropping tears ?

Be quiet, poor heart ! Are the lessons
    Life sets thee so hard to attain
That thou know'st not their potentest essence
    Lies wrapped in the problem of pain ?
Even Nature such rudiments teaches ;—
    The birth-throe presages the breath ;
The soul so high destined, reaches
    Its highest through death.

No beaker is brimmed without bruising
    The clusters that gladden the vine ;
No gem, glitters star-like, refusing
    The rasp that uncovers its shine ;
The diver must dare the commotion
    Of billows above him that swirl,
Ere he from the depths of the ocean
    Can bring up the pearl.

And He, who is molding the spirit,
  Through disciplines changeful and sore,
That so it be fit to inherit
  The marvelous heirship in store—
He measures the weight He is piling,
  He tempers the surge with a touch,
There'll not be a graze of His filing
    Too little, too much.

O heart, canst thou trust Him ? For sake of
  Attainment the noblest, the best,
Content thee awhile to partake of
    These trials so wisely impressed ;
Nor question God's goodness, nor falter,
  Nor say that Thy service is vain,
If *He* bids thee bring to His altar
    Oblations of pain.

Margaret J. Preston.

A LITTLE bird flew my window by,
  'Twixt the level street and the level sky,
The level rows of houses tall,
The long low sun on the level wall ;
And all that the little bird did say
Was, " Over the hills and far away."

A little bird sings above my bed,
And I know if I could but lift my head

I would see the sun set, round and grand,
Upon level sea and level sand,
While beyond the misty distance gray
Is "Over the hills and far away."

I think that a little bird will sing
Over a grassy mound next spring,
Where something that *once* was *me*, ye'll leave ·
In the level sunshine, morn and eve :
But I shall be gone, past night, past day,
"Over the hills and far away."

MISS MULOCK.

I THOUGHT to work for Him. "Master," I said,
"Behold how wide the fields, and the good seed
How few to sow. For Thee all toil were sweet—
Oh, bid me go." He stayed my eager feet.
"Not *that*, my child, the task I have for thee."

"Thou seest, Lord, how white the harvest bends,
How worn the reapers are. Their cry ascends
For help, more help, to garner up the grain—
Here am I, Lord ; send me." Alas, in vain !
The Master saith, "Let others bind the sheaves."

" Thy lambs, dear Lord, are straying from the fold.
Their feet are stumbling o'er the mountains cold—
Far in the night I hear their piteous cry—
Let me bring back the wanderers ere they die."
" No ; other hands must lead them home again."

" Dear Master, dost Thou see the bitter tears
The mourners shed ? Through all the long sad years
Their wails ascend.   Wilt thou not bid me say,
Thy hand shall wipe each mourner's tears away."
" My child, I know their griefs, and I will heal."

" 'Tis not for thee to sow the deathless seed,
Nor thine to bind the sheaves; nor thine to lead
The lost lambs back into their fold again,
Nor yet to soothe the sore heart crushed with pain ;
For thee, my child, another task is set."

And then He led me to my darkened room,
And there amid the silence and the gloom,
My task I found.   But I am well content
To bear the pain and weakness He hath sent,
Rejoiced that I can suffer for His sake.

FATHER, I *must* " lean hard,"
    And lay on Thee the burden of this pain ;
This murmuring impatience too—thou know'st
Is harder still to bear.   My fainting heart

Must find its shelter 'neath the circling arms
Of thine own deep love. Firm, clasp it there !
Take *all* my burden—thou said'st it shall be thine;
Leaning on thee, I know I shall be strong.
Father ! dear Father ! I would be closer yet ;
But thou must draw me, else I cannot come.
Thine *arm* is not enough—where else can I repose
But on thy loving breast ? Soft pillowed there
Forever let me lie ! Weary and weak,
My feet had stumbled on this rugged way,
Had'st thou not held my hand ; and now I'm come
Close to the narrow stream—e'en should its waters
Roar and waves swell high—thine everlasting arms
Shall bear me safely through—its floods can ne'er
O'erwhelm. Father, thou lov'st thy child—
I do not doubt—but *will* " lean hard."

A LL the day long 1 seem to float away
    Through the gray mists that hide both sea and
        sun,
I hear the plash of waves ; I feel their spray,
    And still my boat is drifting farther on.

Love cannot reach me ; death and night alone
    Are with me and with ever-deepening shade
Curtain me 'round, till darkness thick has grown,
    And helpless hands are stretched in vain for aid.

God has forgotten ; only pain has life,
  And weakness, stealing soul and sense away,
God has forgotten, and amid the strife
  I hear the unknown sea and feel its spray.

Faint through the darkness shines a tender light ;
  Soft falls a voice I cannot help but hear—
" *Through waters deep thou passest, yet thy sight*
  Full soon shall know, thy Lord was always
  near."

                                HELEN CAMPBELL.

O SUDDEN blast, that through this silence black
      Sweeps past my windows,
Coming and going with invisible track
      As death or sin does,—

Why scare me, lying sick, and, save thine own,
      Hearing no voices ?
Why mingle with a helpless human moan
      Thy mad rejoicings ?

Why not come gently, as good angels come
      To souls departing,
Floating among the shadows of the room
      With eyes light-darting,

Bringing faint airs of balm that seem to rouse
Thoughts of a far land,
Then binding softly upon weary brows
Death's poppy garland ?

O fearful blast, I shudder at thy sound
Like heathen mortal
Who saw the Three that mark life's doomèd bound
Sit at his portal.

Thou mightst be laden with sad, shrieking souls,
Carried unwilling
From their known earth to the unknown stream that
rolls,
All anguish stilling.

Fierce wind, will the death-angel come like thee,
Soon, soon to bear me
—Whither ? what mysteries may unfold to me,
What terrors scare me ?

Shall I go wandering on, through empty space
As on earth, lonely ?
Or seek through myriad spirit-ranks one face,
And miss that only ?

Shall I then drop down from sphere to sphere
Palsied and aimless ?
Or will my being change so, that both fear
And grief die nameless ?

Rather I pray Him who Himself is love,

. . . .

That even His brightness may not quite efface
    The soul's earth-features,
That in the dear human likeness each may trace
    Glorified creatures ;

That we may not cease loving, only taught
    Holier desiring ;
More faith, more patience ; with more wisdom
    fraught,
    Higher aspiring.

. . . .

Then, strong Azrael, be thy supreme call
    Soft as spring-breezes,
Or like this blast, whose loud fiend festival
    My heart's blood freezes,

I will not fear thee. If thou safely keep
    My soul, God's giving,
And my soul's soul, I, wakening from death-sleep
    Shall first know living.

                           Miss Mulock.

THE Lord knoweth when each hot tear floweth
  From eyes of those who suffer while they pray;
He knows their sorrow, in the glad to-morrow
  Will wipe in gentleness those drops away.

The Lord knoweth when the slow pulse showeth,
That we are drawing near to Jordan's strand,
When our heart faileth, then His strength availeth,
And brings us safely to the better land.

The Lord knoweth ! If your faint heart troweth,
It is uncared for by its God above,
Oh, doubt no longer, but in this be stronger,
He knoweth all things, and His name is Love.

G. Z. G.

PAIN'S furnace-heat within me quivers,
God's breath upon the fire doth blow,
And all my heart in anguish shivers,
And trembles at the fiery glow ;
And yet I whisper, " As God will ! "
And in His hottest fire hold still.

He comes, and lays my heart, all heated,
On the bare anvil, minded so
Into His own fair shape to beat it,
With His great hammer, blow on blow ;
And yet I whisper, " As God will ! "
And at His heaviest blows hold still.

He takes my softened heart and beats it.
The sparks fly off at every blow.
He turns it o'er and o'er, and heats it,
And lets it cool and makes it glow.
And yet I whisper, " As God will ! "
And in His mighty hand hold still.

Why should I murmur ? for the sorrow
Thus only longer-lived would be ;
Its end may come, and will, to-morrow,
When God has done His work in me :
So I say trusting, " As God will ! "
And trusting to the end, hold still.

He kindles for my profit purely,
Affliction's fiery, glowing brand ;
And all his heaviest blows are surely
Inflicted by a master-hand ;
So I say praying, " As God will ! "
And hope in Him, and suffer still.

A LIFE of waiting, lived as for the Lord,
Shall never in his sight be counted lost.
Dost find it hard to wait ?   Remember *this*,
Our will, opposing God's will, makes the cross.

God's plans are great and deep, His ways are wide ;
We strive in vain His will to understand,
Till, looking upward through the mist of doubt,
We hear His loving voice, and clasp His hand.

The reason here we may not understand
Why He should bid some labor, others rest ;
But since His love and wisdom cannot fail,
We know His ways are right, His plans are best.

CONTENT thee—so the angel saith,—
Thy minor makes the triumph strain
Sound sweeter on celestial breath—
And God has use for all thy pain.
His joy thy struggling soul may reach ;
From the strong slain comes sweetness still.
And God lets suffering only teach
Some best revealings of His will.

IF thou, impatient, do let slip thy cross,
Thou wilt not find it in this world again,
Nor in another ; *here and here alone*
Is given thee to suffer for God's sake.
In other worlds we shall more perfectly
Serve Him, and love Him, praise Him, work for
Him,

Grow nearer and nearer Him with all delight ;
But then we shall not any more be called
To suffer, which is our appointment here.
Canst thou not suffer then one hour—or two ?
If He should call thee from thy cross to-day,
Saying, " It is finished ! "—that hard cross of thine
From which thou prayest for deliverance,
Thinkst thou not some passion of regret
Would overcome thee ? Thou wouldst say, "So soon ?
Let me go back, and suffer yet awhile
More patiently—I have not yet praised God."
And He might answer to thee—" Never more.
All pain is done with." Whensoe'er it comes,
That summons that we look for, it will seem
Soon, yea, too soon. Let us take heed in time
That God may now be glorified in us ;
And while we suffer, let us set our souls
To suffer perfectly ; since this alone,—
The suffering, which is this world's special grace,
May here be perfected, and left behind.

From UGO BASSI'S *Sermon.*

" LORD, a little, little longer ! "
Sobs the earth-love, growing stronger,
He will miss me, and go mourning through his soli-
tary days,
And heaven were scarcely heaven,
If these lambs which thou hast given
Were to slip out of our keeping and be lost in the
world's ways.

Lord, it is not fear of dying,
Nor an impious denying
Of Thy will, which forevermore on earth, in heaven,
    be done;
But the love that desperate clings
Unto these, my precious things
In the beauty of the daylight, and the glory of the
    sun.

Ah, Thou still art calling, calling,
With a soft voice unappalling;
And it vibrates in far circles through the everlasting
    years ;
When Thou knockest, even so !
I will arise and go.—

   .   .   .   .   .   .

Miss Mulock.

THOU, who so long has pressed the couch of pain,
   Oh welcome, welcome back to life's free breath,
To life's free breath and day's sweet light again,
   From the chill shadows of the gate of death !

For thou hadst reached the twilight bound between
   The world of spirits and this grosser sphere ;
Dimly by thee the things of earth were seen,
   And faintly fell earth's voices on thine ear.

   .   .   .   .

Thou wert not weary of thy lot ; the earth
   Was ever good and pleasant in thy sight ;
Still clung thy loves about the household hearth,
   And sweet was every day's returning light.

Then welcome back to all thou wouldst not leave,
   To this grand march of seasons, days and hours ;
The glory of the morn, the glow of eve,
   The beauty of the streams and stars and flowers.
   .   .   .   .   .   .

Thou bring'st no tidings of the better land,
   Even from its verge; the mysteries opened there
Are what the faithful heart may understand
   In its still depths, yet words may not declare.

And well I deem, that from the brighter side
   Of life's dim border, some o'erflowing rays
Streamed from the inner glory, shall abide
   Upon thy spirit through the coming days.
   .   .   .   .   .   .

Now may we keep thee from the balmy air
   And radiant walks of heaven a little space,
Where He, who went before thee to prepare
   For his meek followers, shall assign thy place.

WILLIAM CULLEN BRYANT.

XI.

SONGS IN BEREAVEMENT.

" Let us go in and see how the dead rest ! "

" Ah ! I believe there is no *away ;* that no love, no
life, goes ever from us ; it goes as *He* went, that it may
come again, deeper and closer and surer, to be with us
always—even to the end of the world."

" O solitary love ! thou art so strong,
I think God will take pity on thee ere long,
And take thee where thou'lt find those angel faces fair."

SONGS IN BEREAVEMENT.

H E who died at Azan sends
  This to comfort all his friends.
Faithful friends ! It lies, I know,
Pale and white and cold as snow ;
And ye say, " Abdallah's dead ! "
Weeping at the feet and head,
I can see your falling tears,
I can hear your sighs and prayers ;
Yet I smile and whisper this—
" I am not the thing you kiss ;
Cease your tears and let it lie ;
It was mine, it is not ' I.' "

Sweet friends ! what the women lave
For its last bed, called the grave,
Is a hut which I am quitting,
Is a garment no more fitting,

Is a cage from which at last
Like a bird, my soul has passed ;
Love the inmate, not the room ;
The wearer, not the garb ; the plume
Of the falcon, not the bars
Which kept him from those splendid stars !

Loving friends ! be wise and dry
Straightway every weeping eye :
What ye lift upon the bier
Is not worth a wistful tear.
'Tis an empty sea-shell—one
Out of which the pearl has gone :
The shell is broken—it lies there ;
The pearl, the all, the soul is here.
'Tis an earthen jar whose lid
Allah sealed, the while it hid
That treasure of its treasury,
A mind that loved him ; let it lie !
Let the shard be earth's once more;
Since the gold shines in his store !

Allah glorious ! Allah good !
Now thy world is understood ;
Now the long, long wonder ends !
Yet ye weep, my erring friends,
While the man whom ye call dead,
In unspoken bliss, instead,
Lives and loves you ; lost, 'tis true,
By such light as shines for you ;

But in light ye cannot see
´Of unfilled felicity—
In enlarging Paradise—
Lives a life that never dies.

Farewell, friends ! Yet not farewell ;
Where I am, ye too shall dwell.
I am gone before your face
A moment's time, a little space ;
When ye come where I have stepped,
Ye will wonder why ye wept ;
Ye will know by wise love taught,
That here is all, and there is naught.
Weep awhile, if ye are fain—
Sunshine still must follow rain—
Only not at death; for death
Now we know, is that first breath
Which our souls draw when we enter
Life, which is of life the centre.

Be ye certain all seems love
Viewed from Allah's throne above ;
Be ye stout of heart and come
Bravely onward to your home !
La-il Allah ! Allah-la !
O Love divine ! O Love alway !

He who died at Azan gave
This to those who made his grave.

EDWIN ARNOLD.

———Know that his dear children cannot die,
But gently lapsing to an ampler life
Through the brief sleep we misname death, awake
In His most glorious likeness.

SHOULD bereavement's heavy shadow
    Pall-like clothe thy stricken heart,
And the very stars above thee
    Cease their lessons to impart,
Think the dear ones, whose departure
    Round thy soul such darkness cast,
Somewhere find the heavenly morning
    That may rise on thee at last.

OUR prince has gone to his inheritance !
    Think it not strange.   What if, with slight
        half smile,
Some crowned king to leave his throne should
        chance,
    And try the rough ways of the world awhile ?

Ere he had wearied of its storm and stress,
    Would he not hasten to his own again ?
Why should he bear its labor and duress,
    And all the untold burden of its pain ?

Or what if from the golden palace gate
  The king's fair son on some bright morn should
        stray ?
Would he not send his lords of high estate
  To lead him back ere fell the close of day ?

JULIA C. R. DORR.

————WHEN you see a soul set free
From this poor seed of its mortality,
And know you saw not that which is to be,
      Watch you about the tomb
      For its immortal bloom ?

Search for your flowers in the celestial grove :
Look for your precious stream of human love
In the unfathomable sea above :
      Follow your missing bird
      Where songs are always heard !

PHŒBE CARY.

IF for a time some loved one goes away,
  And leaves us our appointed work to do,
  Can we to him or to ourselves be true
In mourning his departure day by day
      And so our work delay ?

Nay, if we love and honor, we shall make
  The absence brief by doing well our task—
Not for ourselves, but for the dear one's sake !
  And at his coming only of him ask
    Approval of the work, which most was done ;
    Not for ourselves, but our belovèd one.

Our Father's house I know is broad and grand ;
  In it how many, many mansions are !
And far beyond the light of sun or star,
Four little ones of mine, through that fair land
  Are walking hand in hand !
Think you I love not, or that I forget
  These of my loins ?   Still this world is fair,
And I am singing while my eyes are wet
  With weeping in this balmy summer air :
    I am not homesick, and the children *here*
    Have need of me, and so my way is clear.

I would be joyful as my days go by,
  Counting God's mercies to me.   He who bore
Life's heaviest cross is mine forevermore,
And I, who wait His coming, shall not I
  On His sure word rely ?
So if sometimes the way be rough, and sleep
  Be heavy for the grief He sends to me,
Or at my waking I would only weep—
  Let me be mindful these are things to be,
    To work His blessèd will until He come,
    And take my hand and lead me safely home.
                              A. D. F. RANDOLPH.

GOD keeps a niche
In Heaven, to hold our idols ; and albeit
He brake them to our faces, and denied
That our close kisses should impair their white,—
I know we shall behold them raised, complete,
The dust swept from their beauty.   .   .

E. B. BROWNING.

NO bird-song floated down the hill,
The tangled bank below was still ;

No rustle from the birchen stem,
No ripples from the water's hem.

The dusk of twilight round us grew,
We felt the falling of the dew ;

For from us, ere the day was done,
The wooded hills shut out the sun.

But on the river's farther side,
We saw the hill-tops glorified :

A tender glow, exceeding fair,
A dream of day without its glare,

With us the damp, the chill, the gloom,
With them the sunset's rosy bloom :

While dark through willowy vistas seen,
The river rolled in shade between,

From out the darkness, where we trod,
We gazed upon those hills of God,

Whose light seemed not of moon or sun ;
We spake not, but our thought was one.

We paused, *as if from that bright shore*
Beckoned our dear ones gone before ;

And stilled our beating hearts to hear
The voices lost to mortal ear !

Sudden our pathway turned from night ;
The hills swung open to the light ;

Thro' their green gates the sunshine showed
A long, slant splendor downward flowed.

Down glade, and glen, and bank it rolled ;
It bridged the shaded stream with gold,

And, borne on piers of mist, allied
The shadowy with the sunlit side !

" So," prayed we, " when our feet draw near
The river, dark with mortal fear,

And the night cometh, chill with dew,
O Father ! let thy light break through !

So let the hills of doubt divide,
So bridge with faith the sunless tide !

So let the eyes that fail on earth
On Thy eternal hills look forth;

And, in Thy beckoning angels, know
The dear ones whom we loved below ! "

WHITTIER.

ONCE, in the twilight of a wintry day,
One passed me silent, struggling on his way,
With head bowed low, and hands that burdens bore,
And saw not how, a little space before,

A woman watched his coming, where the light
Poured a glad welcome through a window bright,
Set thick with flowers that showed no fairer bloom
Than her sweet face, turned outward to the gloom.

Yet when his foot, with quick, impatient stride,
But touched the step, the door swung open wide,
Soft hands reached swiftly out, with eager hold,
And drew the dear one in from storm and cold.

O love ! whose eyes, from some celestial height,
Behold me toiling, burdened through the night,
Tender of every blast at which I cower,
Yet smiling still, to know how brief the hour ;

Keeping within thy radiant, love-lit home,
Some glad surprise to whisper when I come—
'Tis but a breath till I the door shall win,
And thy dear hands will swiftly draw me in !

EMILY HUNTINGDON MILLER.

SOULS that of His own good life partake,
    He loves as His own self ; dear as His eye
They are to Him : He'll never them forsake :
    When they shall die, then God Himself shall die :
    They live, they live in blest eternity.

HENRY MORE.

.   .   . Now I need not fear for thee,
    Where thou art, all is well ;
For thou thy Father's face doth see,
    With Jesus thou dost dwell !
Yes, cloudless joys around him shine,
His heart shall never ache like mine ;
He sees the radiant armies glow
That keep and guide us here below.

He hears their singing evermore,
 His little voice too sings,
He drinks of wisdom deepest love,
 He speaks of secret things,
That we can never see or know
Howe'er we seek or strive below,
While yet amid the mists we stand
That veil this dark and tearful land.

O that I could but watch afar,
 And hearken but awhile
To that sweet song that hath no jar,
 And see his heavenly smile.
As he doth praise the holy God
Who made him pure for that abode !
In tears of joy full well I know
This burdened heart would overflow.

And I should say : Stay here, my son,
 My wild laments are o'er,
O well for thee that thou hast won,
 I call thee back no more,
But come, thou fiery chariot, come !
And bear me swiftly to thy home,
Where he with many a loved one dwells,
And evermore of gladness tells.

Then be it as my Father wills,
 I will not weep for thee ;
Thou livest, joy thy spirit fills
 Pure sunshine thou dost see,

The sunshine of eternal rest ;
.Abide my child where thou art blest;
I with our friends will onward fare,
And when God wills, shall find thee there.

PAUL GERHARDT, 1650.

I HAVE no moan to make,
No bitter tears to shed ;
No heart, that for rebellious grief
Will not be comforted.

There is no friend of mine
Laid in the earth to sleep,—
No grave so green or heaped afresh
By which I stand and weep.

Though some, whose presence once
Sweet comfort 'round me shed,
Here in the body walk no more
The way that I must tread.

Not they, but what they wore
Went to the house of fear,—
They, were the incorruptible,
They left corruption here.

The veil of flesh that hid,
  Is softly drawn aside,
More clearly I behold them now
  Than those who never died.

Who died ! what means that word,
  Of men so much abhorred ?
Caught up in clouds of heaven to be
  Forever with the Lord !

To give this body, racked
  With mortal ills and cares,
For one as glorious and as fair
  As our Redeemer wears.

To leave our shame and sin,
  Our hunger and disgrace ;
To come unto ourselves, to turn
  And find our Father's face.

To run, to leap, to walk ;—
  To quit our beds of pain ;
And live where the inhabitants
  Are never sick again.

To sit no longer dumb,
  Nor halt nor blind ; to rise ;
To praise the Healer with our tongue,
  And see Him with our eyes.

To leave cold winter snows,
  And burning summer heats ;
And walk in soft, white, tender light,
  About the golden streets.

Thank God for all *my* loved
  That, out of pain and care,
Have safely reached the heavenly hights,
  And stay to meet me there !

Not these I mourn, I know
  Their joy by faith sublime—
But for myself, that still below
  Must wait my appointed time.

PHŒBE CARY.

GOOD night ! good night ! as we so oft have said
    Beneath this roof at midnight, in the days
  That are no more, and shall no more return,
Thou has but taken thy lamp and gone to bed ;
  I stay a little longer, as one stays
  To cover up the embers that still burn.

LONGFELLOW.

IT sometimes happens that two friends will meet,
  And, with a smile and touch of hands, again
Go on their way along the noisy street.
Each is so sure of all the friendship sweet,
  The loving silence gives no thought of pain.

And so, I think, those friends whom we call dead
    Are with us. It may be some quiet hour,
Or time of busy work for hand or head—
Their love fills all the heart that missed them so.
    They bring a sweet assurance of the life
Serene, above the worry that we know ;
    And we grow braver for the comfort brought.
Why should we mourn because they do not speak
    Our words that lie so far below their thought ?

Sunday Afternoon.

WHAT to shut eyes has God revealed ?
    What hear the ears that death has sealed ?
What undreamed beauty, passing show,
Requites the loss of all we know ?

O silent land, to which we move,
Enough if there alone be love ;
And mortal need can ne'er outgrow
What it is waiting to bestow !

O white soul ! from that far-off shore
Float some sweet song the waters o'er ;
Our faith confirm, our fears dispel,
With the old voice we loved so well !

Whittier.

I SIT beside the sea this autumn day,
    When sky and tide are ravishingly blue,
And melt into each other.   Down the bay,
The stately ships drift by so still and slow,
That on the horizon's verge I scarce may know
Which be the sails along the wave that glow,
    And which the clouds that float the azure through.

From beds of golden-rod and asters, steal
    The south winds, soft as any breath of May ;
High in the sunny air the white gulls wheel,
As noiseless as the clouds they poise below;
And in the hush the white waves come and go,
As if a spell entranced them, and their flow
    Echoed the beat of oceans far away.

O loved and lost ! can you not stoop to me
    This perfect morn, when heaven and earth are
    one ?
The south winds breathe of you ; I only see
(Alas the vision sweet can naught avail !)
Your image in the cloud, the wave, the sail ;
And heed nor calm, nor storm, nor bliss nor bale,
    Remembering you have gone beyond the sun.

One look into your eyes; one clasp of hands:
    One murmured, " Lo I love you as before ; "
And I would give you to your viewless lands

And wait my time, with never tear or sigh;—
But not a whisper comes from earth or sky,
And the sole answer to my yearning cry,
   Is the faint wash of waves along the shore.

Lord, dost Thou see how dread a thing is death?
   When silence such as this is all it leaves?
To watch in agony the parting breath
Till the fond eyes are closed, the dear voice still,
And know that not the wildest prayer can thrill
Thee, to awake them, but our grief must fill
   Alike the rosy morns, the rainy eves.

Ah! Thou *dost* see; and not a pang is vain!—
   Some joy of every anguish must be born;
Else this one planet's weight of loss and pain
Would stay the stars in sympathetic woe,
And make the suns move pale and cold and slow,
Till all was black and void, the throne below,
   And night shut down without a gleam of morn.

But mark! The sun goes radiant to his goal
   While winds make music on the laughing sea;
And with his set, the starry host will roll
Celestial splendors over mead and main;
Lord, can Thy worlds be glad and death enchain?
Nay! 'tis but crowning for immortal reign
   In the pure realm where all abide with thee.

What star has seen the sun at cloudless noon !
What chrysalis knows aught of wings that soar ?
O blessed souls ! how can I hope the boon
Of look or word from you, the glorified,
Until for me the shining gates swing wide ?—
Welcome the day when the great deeps divide,
And we are one, in life forever more.

EDENA DEAN PROCTOR.

"WOULD that I too were lying
    Beneath the churchyard sod
With my limbs at rest in the green earth's breast,
And my soul at home with God."

I never lay me down to sleep at night
But in my heart I sing that little song :
The angels hear it, as a pitying throng,
They touch my burning lids with fingers, bright
As moonbeams, pale, impalpable, and light;

And when my daily pious tasks are done,
And all my patient prayers said one by one,
God hears it.   Seems it sinful in his sight
That round my slow burnt offering, of quenched
        will,
One quivering human sigh creeps, wind-like, still ?

That when my orisons celestial fail
Rises one note of natural human wail ?
.   .   .   . Ere long
I trust God will forgive my singing that poor song.

A year ago I bade a little one
Bear upon pilgrimage a heavy load
Of alms ; he cried, half fainting on the road,
" Weary, O weary, would the day were done ! "
Him I reproved with tears, and said, "Go on !
Nor pause, nor murmur till thy task be o'er—"
Would not God say the same to me, and more ?

I will not sing that song ! Thou dearest one,
.   .   .   .   . Stretch thy steadfast hand
And let mine grasp it. Now I also, stand,
My woman weakness nerved to strength like thine ;
We'll quaff life's aloe-cup as if 'twere wine
Each to the other; journeying on apart,
Till at heaven's golden doors we two leap heart to
    heart.

JEAN INGELOW.

T HEY never quite leave us—the friends who have
        passed
    Through the shadows of death to the sunlight above ;
A thousand sweet memories are holding them fast
    To the places they blessed with their presence and
    love.

The work which they left and the books which they
   read
Speak mutely, though still with an eloquence rare,
And the songs that they sung, and dear words they
   said,
Still linger and sigh on the desolate air.

And oft when alone, and as oft in the throng
   Or when evil allures us, or sin draweth nigh,
A whisper comes gently, " Nay, do not the wrong,"
   And we feel that our weakness is pitied on high.

In the dew-threaded morn and the opaline eve,
   When the children are merry, or crimsoned with
      sleep,
We are comforted, even as lonely we grieve,
   For the thought of their rapture forbids us to weep.

We toil at our task in the burden and heat
   Of life's passionate noon.   They are folded in peace.
It is well.   We rejoice that their heaven is sweet,
   And one day for us all the bitter will cease.

We, too, will go home o'er the river of rest
   As the strong and the lovely before us have gone.
Our sun will go down in the beautiful west,
   To rise in the glory that circles the throne.

Until then we are bound by our love and our faith
  To the saints who are walking in Paradise fair :
They have passed beyond sight, at the touching of
    death,
  But they live like ourselves, in God's infinite care.

MARGARET E. SANGSTER.

OH, blessèd are the dead !
    Why will we mourn for them ?
No more the stormy billows here
    With weary heart they stem !
No more they struggle here below
To guide, through many a gulf of woe,
    Their being's fragile bark ;
But harbored in eternal rest,
By far-off islands of the blest,
Calm on a sunlit ocean's breast,
    Anchor their fearless ark.

Seem they to sleep ? 'tis but as sleeps
    The seed within the earth,
To burst forth to the brilliant morn
    Of a more glorious birth ;
Seem they to feel no breath of love
That o'er their icy brow will move
    With tearful whispers warm ?

'Tis that upon their spirit's ear
All Heaven's triumphant music clear
Is bursting, where there comes not near
One tone of sorrow's storm !

Oh ! give them up to Him, whose own
Those dear redeemed ones are !
Lo ! on their wakening souls He breaks
  ' The bright and morning star ! '
His are they now, for evermore,—
The mystery and the conflict o'er,
  The Eternal City won !
As conquerors let them pass and go
Up from the fight of faith below,
The peace of God at last to know
  In kingdoms of the sun !

ELIZA MARY HAMILTON.

STILL always groweth in me the great wonder,
  When all the fields are blushing like the dawn,
And only one poor little flower ploughed under,
  That I can see no flowers, that *one* being gone :
  No flower of all, because of one being gone.

Aye, ever in me groweth the great wonder,
  When all the hills are shining, white and red,
And only one poor little flower ploughed under,
  That it were all as one if all were dead.

          .   .   .   .

I cannot feel the beauty of the roses ;
  Their soft leaves seem to me but layers of dust ;
Out of my opening hand each blessing closes :
  Nothing is left me but my hope and trust,
  Nothing but heavenly hope and heavenly trust.

I get no sweetness of the sweetest places ;
  My house, my friends no longer comfort me ;
Strange somehow grow the old familiar faces ;
  For I can nothing have, not having thee.

Having, I have them not—strange contradiction !
  Heaven needs must cast its shadow on our earth;
Yea, drown us in the waters of affliction
  Breast high, to make us know our treasure's worth,
  To make us know how much our love is worth.

And while I mourn, the anguish of my story
  Breaks, as the wave breaks on the hindering bar :
Thou art but hidden in the deeps of glory,
  Even as the sunshine hides the lessening star.
  And with true love, I love thee from afar.

I know our Father must be good, not evil,
And murmur not, for faith's sake, at my ill ;
Nor at the mystery of the working cavil,
That somehow bindeth all things in His will,
And, though He slay me, makes me trust Him
still.

ALICE CARY.

SAYING, " There is no hope," he stepped
A little from our side and passed
To hope eternal.   At the last,
Crying, " There is no rest," he slept.

A sweeter spirit ne'er drew breath ;
Strange grew the chill upon the air,
But as he murmured, " This is death,"
Lo ! life itself did meet him there.

He loved the Will ; he did the deed.
Such love shall live.   Such doubt is dust.
He served the truth ; he missed the creed.
Trust him to God.   Dear is the trust.

ELIZABETH STUART PHELPS.

STRANGE, strange for thee and me,
    Sadly afar ;
Thou safe beyond, above,
    I 'neath the star;
Thou where flowers deathless spring,
    I where they fade ;
Thou in God's paradise,
    I 'mid time's shade !

Thou where each gale breathes balm,
    I tempest tossed ;
Thou where true joy is found,
    I where 'tis lost ;
Thou counting ages thine,
    I not the morrow ;
Thou learning more of bliss,
    I more of sorrow.

Thou in eternal peace,
    I 'mid earth's strife ;
Thou where care hath no name,
    I where 'tis life ;
Thou without need of hope,
    I where 'tis vain ;
Thou with wings dropping light,
    I with time's chain.

Strange, strange for thee and me,
    Loved, loving ever ;
Thou by Life's deathless fount,
    I near Death's river ;

Thou winning Wisdom's love,
　　I strength to trust ;
Thou 'mid the seraphim,
　　I in the dust !

PHŒBE CARY.

SHE shut the door and turned away,
　　Some task was waiting for her hand ;
She shut another door, where lay
　　Her sweet dead hope,—you understand ?
" And they shall weep no more," God saith.
" Nor taste of pain." Oh, Life ! Oh, Death !

HATTIE TYNG GRISWOLD.

GO not far in the land of light !
　　A little while by the golden gate,
Lest that I lose you out of sight,
　　Wait, my darling, wait.

Forever now from your happy eyes
　　Life's scenic picture has passed away;
You have entered into realities,
　　And I am yet at the play !

.　　.　　.　　.　　.　　.　　.　　.　　.

But the last sad act is drawing on ;
A little while by the golden gate
Of the holy heaven to which you are gone,
Wait, my darling, wait.

ALICE CARY.

THERE'S not an hour but from some sparkling
    beach
Go joyful men, in fragile ships, to sail
By unknown seas to unknown lands. They hail
The freshening winds with eager hope and speech
Of wondrous countries which they soon will reach.
Left on the shore, we wave our hands, with pale,
Wet cheeks, but hearts that are ashamed to quail
Or own the grief which selfishness would teach.
Oh ! Death, the fairest lands beyond thy sea
Lie waiting, and thy barks are swift and stanch
And ready.   Why do we reluctant launch ?
And when our friends their heritage have claimed
Of thee, and entered on it, rich and free,
Oh ! why of sorrow are we not ashamed ?

HELEN JACKSON.

IF, as we dream, in every radiant star
   We see a shining gate through which the soul
In its degrees of being, will ascend—
If, when these weary organs drop away

We shall forget their uses and commune
With angels and each other, as the stars
Mingle their light in silence and in love—
What is this fleshly fetter of a day
That we should bind it with immortal flowers !
How do we ever gaze upon the sky,
And watch the lark soar up till he is lost,
And turn to our poor perishing dreams away,
Without one tear for our imprisoned wings !

N. P. WILLIS,

XII.

SONGS IN DEATH.

" Shall we follow the Hand that guides us on our long unknown journey, with less of gladness and confident trust than the birds who cross leagues of sea guided by the same Hand?"

" To pass through the valley of the shadow of death is the way home."

" As in this life we woke into consciousness in the arms of friends, so we may venture to hope that our next waking will be bosomed by that Eternal Love which provided for this shelter here."

SONGS IN DEATH.

" How are the dead raised up, and with what body do they come ? "

THE waves, they are wildly heaving
  And bearing me out from the shore,
And I know of the things I am leaving,
  But not of the things before.
O Lord of Love, whom the shape of a dove
  Came down and hovered o'er,
Descend to-night with heavenly light,
  And show me the farther shore.

There is midnight darkness o'er me,
  And 'tis light, more light, I crave ;
The billows behind and before me
  Are gaping each with a grave ;
Descend to-night, O Lord of might,
  Who died our souls to save ;
Descend to-night, my Lord, my Light,
  And walk with me on the wave !

My heart is heavy to breaking
  Because of the mourners' sighs,
For they cannot see the awak'ning
  Nor the body with which we arise.
Thou, who for sake of men didst break
  The awful seal of the tomb—
Show *them* the way into life, I pray,
  And the body with which we come!

Comfort their pain and pining
  For the nearly wasted sands,
With the many mansions shining
  In the house not made with hands:
And help them by faith to see through death
  To that brighter and better shore,
Where they never shall weep who are fallen asleep,
  And never be sick any more.

ALICE CARY.

"Break, O Morning of the Everlasting Day!"

SEE how the far east brightens!
  Hear ye the angels singing,
Through morning's fresh'ning breath?
No darkness longer frightens:
Now, rich with mercy, bringing
Your help, comes gracious Death.

Then give him friendly greeting,
He will be friendly too,
And bring, each joy completing,
His olden bliss to you.

To him—whose near end stealing
Through heart and limb presages night,—
Who kneeling,
Who kneeling, sure appealing,
Turns soul and hands
Where Mercy stands,
The Lord will make it light.

Tr. from Fouqué, *by* Andrews.

I AM going away, dear friend,
  Away to a brighter land ;
And even now, as the shadows fall,
I wait the voice of the Angel's call
    And the touch of the Angel's hand.

The way hath been long, dear friend,
    Weary and long and lone ;
And oh ! the pain of the wounded heart,
The silent pang and the secret smart !
    May they never to *thee* be known.

Yet bright was the prospect, friend,
    When the path before me lay ;
When love's sweet blossoms were round my feet,
And the far-off future lay clear and sweet
    In the flush of rising day.

Oh ! beautiful dreams of youth !
    Oh ! visions that fade so soon !
And oh ! the desolate, dreary way,
When back we look through the darkened day
    To the sun that set ere noon.

But the journey at last is o'er
    And the struggle and toil are past ;
And the holy angels who led me on
Till the fight was fought and the victory won,
    They have brought me home at last.

Home, to an endless rest ;
    Home to my Father—God ;
And I bless his name, that through wrong and loss,
I have borne the weight of the iron cross,
    And the thorny path have trod.

Oh ! sweet is the thought and strange,
    That so near unto Him I stand ;
That ere the shadows of night shall close
I shall drink of the River of Life that flows
    In the beautiful Spirit Land !

That my mother's hand I shall clasp
  And my father's smile shall see ;
And oh ! the thrill of the glad surprise
When I meet the gaze of the dearest eyes
  That ever gleamed on me !

I know they are near me now ;
  I know that they stand and wait ;
And I feel the flush of a love divine,
And a light as of heaven about me shine
  As I kneel at the golden gate.

And lo ! the gates ajar,
  And the light of immortal day !
I see the angels ; I hear their call ;
And earth falls back like a gloomy pall,
  As they bear my soul away !

SUSAN ARCHER WEISS.

A
T evening time let there be light :
  Life's little day draws near its close ;
Around me fall the shades of night,
  The night of death, the grave's repose :
  To crown my joys, to end my woes,
At evening time let there be light.

Stormy and dark hath been my day,
  Yet rose the morn divinely bright ;
Dews, birds and blossoms cheered the way ;
Oh, for one sweet, one parting ray !
At evening time there *shall* be light ;
For God hath spoken—it must be :
  Fear, doubt and anguish, take their flight,
His glory now is risen on me !
Mine eyes shall his salvation see :
—'Tis evening time, and there *is* light !

JAMES MONTGOMERY.

.   .   .   .   .   As one who peers
Into the dark bewildered, and descries
  A guiding lamp within the casement set,
    Knowing it homeward leads his weary feet,
So I, with yearning heart and wistful eyes,
  As in a vision wonderful and sweet,
    Beyond the grave, behold it shining yet.

ARCHBISHOP LAIGHTON.

. . . .
SHE said : "I am come to heaven at last,
  And I'll do as the blessèd do ! "
But the custom of earth was stronger than Heaven,
  And the habit of life than death,—
How should anguish as old as thought
  Be healed by the end of breath ?

Tissue and nerve and pulse of her soul
Had absorbed the disease of woe.
The strangest of all the angels there
Was Joy (Oh the wretched know !)

.   .   .   .

" I must *learn* to be happy in heaven," she said,
" As we *learned* to suffer below."—

.   .   .   .

But the saddest spirit in the world
Came to herself at last.

ELIZABETH STUART PHELPS.

So let us die ;
Yield up our little lives as the flowers do;
Believing He'll not lose one single soul,—
One germ of his immortal.   Naught of His
Or Him can perish ; therefore let us die.

MISS MULOCK.

LOOK above thee—never eye
    Saw such pleasures as await thee ;
Thought ne'er reached such scenes of joy

As are there prepared to meet thee ;
Light undying, seraph's lyres,
Angel welcomes, cherub choirs,
Smiling through heaven's doors to greet thee.

BOWRING.

I HEAR a voice you cannot hear,
　Which says I must not stay;
I see a hand you cannot see,
　Which beckons me away.

TICKELL.

　．　．　．　．　．　．　．　．

WHAT is that, we call death ?
Is it to drop with all our hopes and fears
Down to the silence of eternal years,
　When ends this laboring breath ?
To have no part in all this wondrous whole,
While suns shall rise and starry heavens roll ?
　Is this, what men call death ?

　．　．　．　．　．　．　．　．

Hear what the Master saith :—
" My father's house has mansions large and fair,
Where happy souls released from earthly care,

Shall breathe in heavenly breath ;
So hence I go to make for you a place,
To come again and bring you face to face,
    No more to taste of death."

The ransomed of the Lord
On Zion's clear and holy heights shall tread,
With everlasting joy upon their head,
    And songs in full accord ;
Here joy and gladness ever shall remain,
While far behind them lie the realms of pain :
    God's last and grand reward.

Increase N. Tarbox.

REACH down the wanderer's staff,
    Tie on the sandals on the traveler's feet;
The wan-eyed moon weeps in the watery east;
Gird up the loins and let me now depart!

Frances Kemble Butler.

UNTO Him who washed us
    Whiter than snow
We shall pass through the shallow river
    With hearts aglow.

For the Lord's voice on the water
    Lingereth sweet,
" He that *is* washed, needeth only
    To wash his feet ! "

                B. M.

E ARTH, with its dark and dreadful ills,
    Recedes and fades away ;
Lift up your heads, ye heavenly hills :
    Ye gates of death, give way !

My soul is full of whispered song ;
    My blindness is my sight ;
The shadows that I feared so long
    Are all alive with light.

The while my pulses faintly beat,
    My faith doth so abound,
I feel grow firm beneath my feet
    The green, immortal ground.

That faith to me a courage gives
    Low as the grave to go :
I know that my Redeemer lives,—
    That I shall live I know.

             ALICE CARY.

C LOSE, close, beloved mine,
Around my heart entwine,
In Love's strong clasping, as I hold thee, so.
Above the sky that leans
Over these deathfu' scenes
To Him, the Eternal Life and Love, we go.

V ITAL spark of heavenly flame !
Quit, O quit this mortal frame !
Trembling, hoping, lingering, flying,
O the pain, the bliss of dying !
Cease fond Nature, cease thy strife,
Let me languish into life !

Hark! they whisper; angels say
Sister spirit, come away !
What is this absorbs me quite ?
Steals my senses, shuts my sight,
Drowns my spirits, draws my breath ?
Tell me, my soul, can this be death ?

The world recedes: it disappears!
Heaven opens on my eyes ! my ears
With sounds seraphic ring:
Lend, lend your wings! I mount! I fly!
O Grave ! where is thy victory ?
O Death ! where is thy sting ?

ALEXANDER POPE.

OH, what will be that life to come
   Beyond this vale of tears
To which we pass full soon ?

What will it be ? Oh, tell me pray,
So that my fears may pass away.

Oh, in that life which is to come
   Will there be pain as now ?
Will hearts there ache as they do here,
   Will souls with burdens bow ?
Oh, would that I might know full well
Ere to that land I go to dwell.

Oh, in that life which is to come
   Will there be joy supreme,
And on my path from day to day
   Will light effulgent stream ?
Will flowers bloom with fragrance sweet,
And all sweet things my senses greet ?

Oh, in that life which is to come
   Shall I then clasp the hands
Of those I knew and loved so here ?
   Shall I then join the bands
Of free and happy souls above
Where all is bliss and all is love ?

And no more parting will there be
In that sweet life to come?
Will want and wandering ever end,
And shall we dwell at home
Within a Father's mansion grand,
Protected by His loving hand?

Oh, soul! there comes a voice to thee
Sounding the waters o'er,
In love it says, in truth it says,
" Thou shalt bear grief no more,
And all thy tears be wiped away
When in this land of cloudless day."

For in this land no graves are seen,
No links are snapped in twain,
And they that meet may love for aye
And never part again.
No sickness, pain, or dying here,
No blighted buds or leaflets sere.

Oh, to that land then let me haste,
Borne on the wings of Time;
I long to greet that happy land,
That blest immortal clime,
Where I shall hear the Saviour say
The former things are passed away.

G. W. CROFTS.

THE sands of time are sinking,
The dawn of heaven breaks,
The summer morn I've sighed for,
The fair sweet morn awakes !
Dark, dark hath been the midnight,
But dayspring is at hand,
And glory—glory dwelleth
In Immanuel's land.

Oh, well it is forever !
Oh, well for evermore !
My nest hung in no forest
Of all this death-doomed shore;
Yea, let the vain world vanish,
As from the ship the strand,
While glory—glory dwelleth
In Immanuel's land.

I've wrestled on toward heaven
'Gainst storm and wind and tide:
Now like a weary traveler
That leaneth on his guide,
Amid the shades of evening
While sinks life's lingering sand,
I hail the glory dawning
From Immanuel's land.

With mercy and with judgment
My web of time He wove,
And all the dews of sorrow
Were lustered with His love :

I'll bless the Hand that guided,
I'll bless the Heart that planned,
When throned where glory dwelleth,
In Immanuel's land

TURN the Past's mirror backward. Its shadows
removed,
The dim confused mass becomes softened, sublime :
I have worked—I have felt—I have lived, I have
loved,
And each was a step towards the goal I now climb :
Thou, God, Thou sawest the good of it.

MISS MULOCK.

COME now, all ye terrors ! sally !
Muster forth into the valley,
Where triumphant darkness hovers
With a sable wing, that covers
Brooding horror. Come, thou death,
Let the damps of thy dull breath
Overshadow e'en the shade,
And make darkness' self afraid ;
There, my feet, even there, doth find
Way for a resolvèd mind :
Still, my Shepherd—still, my God,
Thou art with me ; still Thy rod

And Thy staff, whose influence
Gives direction, gives defense.

.   .   .   .   .   .

Lighting the eternities.

.   .   .   .   .   .

Thence my ripe soul will I breathe
Warm into the arms of Death.

                     RICHARD CRASHAW, 1650.

L IFE ! we have been long together,
   Through pleasant and through cloudy weather,
'Tis hard to part when friends are dear,
Perhaps 'twill cost a sigh, a tear.
Then steal away, give little warning.

.   .   .   .

     Say not good night,
     But in some brighter clime
     Bid me good-morning.

                     MRS. BARBAULD.

O N a far shore my land swam far from my sight,
   But I could see familiar, native stars ;
My home was shut from me by ocean bars,
Yet home hung there above me in the night ;

Unchanged fell down on me Orion's light ;
  As always, Venus rose, and fiery Mars ;
  My own the Pleiades yet, and without jars
In wonted tones, sang all the heavenly height ;
So when in death from underneath my feet
  Rolls the round world, I now do see the sky
  Of God's truth, burning yet familiarly ;
My native constellations I can greet ;
  I lose the outer, not the inner eye,
  The landscape, not the soul's stars, as I die.

.   .   .   .   Not in vain do we
Read signals of grander destiny,
And in our exile pine for kingly state.
The sun is but the shadow ; the unseen
Is the true light, and changeless and serene,
Cheers our approach to that mysterious goal
Called death ! which is the daybreak of the soul.

Frances L. Mace, in Independent.

. . . . , .

THE sufferer sings — his end is near ;
  From sin and pain he bursts away,
Trouble shall die this very day !

Tr. from Schmolke by Gurney.

NEVER think of me as lying
  By the dismal mold o'erspread ;
But about the soft white pillow
  Folded underneath my head,
And of summer flowers weaving
  Their rich 'broidery o'er my bed.
Think of the immortal spirit
  Living up above the sky,
And of how my face is wearing
  Light of immortality ;
Looking earthward, is o'erleaning
  The white bastion of the sky.

PHŒBE CARY.

I KNOW not where Thine islands lift
  Their fronded palms in air,
I only know we cannot drift
  Beyond Thy love and care.

WHITTIER.

" HE does well who does his best ;
  Is he weary ? let him rest."
Brothers ! *I have done my best,*
I am weary—let me rest.

After toiling oft in vain,
Baffled, yet to struggle fain ;
After toiling long, to gain
Little good with mickle pain,
Let me rest. But lay me low
Where the hedgeside roses blow ;
Where the little daisies grow,
Where the winds a-Maying go ;
Where the footpath rustics plod ;
Where the breeze-bowed poplars nod ;
Where the old woods worship God,
Where His pencil paints the sod ;
Where the wedded throstle sings,
Where the young bird tries his wings ;
Where the wailing plover swings,
Near the runlet's rushing springs !
Where, at times, the tempest's roar,
Shaking distant sea and shore,
Still will rave old Barnsdale o'er,
To be heard by me no more !
There, beneath the breezy west,
Tired and thankful, let me rest,
Like a child that sleepeth best
On its mother's gentle breast.

WHY weep ye for the falling
    Of the transient twilight gloom ?
I am weary of the journey,
    And have come in sight of home.

I can see a white procession
Sweep melodiously along,
And I would not have your mourning
Drown the sweetness of their song.

The battle strife is ended;
I have scaled the hindering wall,
And I am putting off the armor
Of the soldier—that is all !

Would you hide me from my pleasures ?
Would you hold me from my rest ?
From my serving and my waiting
I am called to be a guest !

Of its heavy, hurtful burdens
Now my spirit is released;
I am done with fasts and scourges,
And am bidden to the feast.

While you see the sun descending,
While you lose me in the night,
Lo, the heavenly morn is breaking,
And my soul is in the light.

I, from faith to sight am rising,
While in deeps of doubt you sink ;
'Tis the glory that divides us,
Not the darkness, as you think.

Then lift up your drooping eyelids,
  And take heart of better cheer ;
'Tis the cloud of coming spirits
  Makes the shadows that ye fear.

O they come to bear me upward
  To the mansions of the sky,
And to change as I am changing
  Is to live, and not to die.

Is to leave the pain, the sickness,
  And the smiting of the rod,
And to dwell among the angels
  In the City of our God.

ALICE CARY.

AND this is death ! Think you that raptured soul
  Now walking humbly in the golden streets,
Bearing the precious burden of a love
Too great for utterance, or with hushed heart
Drinking the music of the ransomed throng,
Counts death an evil ? evil, sickness, pain,
Calamity, or aught that God prescribed
To cure it of its sin, and bring it where
The healing hand of Christ might touch it ? No !
He is a man to-night—a man in Christ.
This was his childhood, here ; and as we give

A smile of wonder to the little woes
That drew the tears from out our own young eyes—
The kind corrections and severe constraints
Imposed by those who loved us—so he sees
A father's chastisement in all the ill
That filled his life with darkness ; so he sees
In every evil a kind instrument
To chasten, elevate, correct, subdue,
And fit him for that heavenly estate—
Saintship in Christ—the Manhood Absolute.

J. G. HOLLAND.

XIII.

THE SONG OF SONGS
AND
"THE NEW SONG."

To be sung Only
When the Night-Songs are Past.

" Then shall the Day dawn, and the Day-star arise in
your hearts."

" And there shall be no Night there ! "

THE SONG OF SONGS.

A SCEND, Beloved to the love;
This is the day of days;
To-night the bridal song is sung,
To-night ten thousand harps are strung
In sympathy with heart and tongue,
  Unto the Lamb's high praise.

The festal lamps are lighting now,
  In the great marriage hall;
By angel hands the board is spread,
By angel hands the sacred bread
Is on the golden table laid ;
  The King his own doth call.

The gems are gleaming from the roof,
  Like stars in night's round dome;
The festal wreaths are hanging there,
The festal fragrance fills the air,
And flowers of heaven divinely fair
  Unfold their happy bloom.

Long, long deferred, now come at last,
   The Lamb's glad wedding day ;
The guests are gathering to the feast,
The seats in heavenly order placed,
The royal throne above the rest;—
   How bright the new array.

Sorrow and sighing are no more,
   The weeping hours are past;
To-night the waiting will be done,
To-night the wedding robe put on,
The glory and the joy begun ;
   The crown has come at last.

Without, within, is light, is light;
   Around, above, is love, is love ;
We enter to go out no more,
We raise the song unsung before,
We doff the sackcloth that we wore,
   For all is joy above.

Ascend, Beloved, to the life ;
   Our days of death are o'er;
Mortality has done its worst,
The fetters of the tomb are burst,
The last has now become the first,
   Forever, evermore.

Ascend, Beloved, to the feast,
Make haste, thy day is come ;
Thrice blessed are they the Lamb doth call,
To share the heavenly festival
In the new Salem's palace halls,
Our everlasting home.

HORATIUS BONAR.

THE NEW SONG.

A BOVE the dissonance of Time,
    And discord of its angry words,
I hear the everlasting chime,
    The music of unjarring chords.

I bid it welcome ; and my haste
    To join it cannot brook delay ;—
O song of morning, come at last,
    And ye who sing it, come away !

O song   of light, and dawn, and bliss,
    Sound over earth, and fill these skies,
Nor ever, ever, ever cease,
    Thy soul entrancing melodies.

Horatius Bonar.

INDEX OF FIRST LINES.

	AUTHOR.	PAGE.
Above the dissonance of time....	Horatius Bonar	286
Across the field of daily work...	William C. Gannett	169
Across the hedges thick with autumn flowers		167
Ah! for the heart that goes	Howard Glyndon	146
Ah, long the storm, yet none the less	Mrs. A. D. T. Whitney	20
Ah me! the ways of God with man	Mary Bradley	27
A life of waiting lived as for the Lord		221
A little bird flew my window by.	Miss Mulock	213
A little bird I am. Prison Hymn of	Madam Guyon	114
All common things, each day's events	Longfellow	179
All is of God! If He but wave His hand	Mrs. A. D. T. Whitney	37
All the day long I seem to float away	Helen Campbell	216
Among so many can He care?....	Mrs. A. D. T. Whitney	149
And is there care in heaven?....	Edmund Spenser	77
And so we yearn and so we sigh..	Mrs. A. D. T. Whitney	35
And this is death! think you that raptured soul	J. G. Holland	279
Ascend, beloved to the love	Horatius Bonar	283
A raveled rainbow overhead	Mrs. A. D. T. Whitney	11
As one who peers	Archbishop Leighton	264
As on wrecked battle grounds....	Adelaide George Bennett	54
As the bird trims her to the gale..	Emerson	144
As the poor panting hart to the waterbrook runs	Alice Cary	167
As torrents in summer. From "The Nun of Nidaros"	Longfellow	52
At evening time let there be light.	James Montgomery	263
Behold the throng	Abraham Perry Miller	122
Be not amazed at life	Dean Alford	153

	AUTHOR.	PAGE.
Be still, my soul, Jehovah loveth thee....................	Horatius Bonar.............	92
Blessed are they who are home-sick.................	Heinrich Stilling...........	56
Blest by whom most the cross is known. Translated from Schmolke by........	Gurney	88
Build thee most stately mansions, O my soul...................	Oliver Wendell Holmes.....	202
But all through life I see a cross.	Olrig Grange	82
But who shall praise God in the night?.....	B. M.................... ...	4
Caught in the bitter net of circumstance		95
Close, close, beloved mine.......		269
Come in, O gracious Form, I say.		107
Come now, all ye terrors! sally!..	Richard Crashaw..........	273
Content thee—so the angel saith—		222
Crush the dead leaves under thy feet.................		51
Dear night! this world's defeat..	Henry Vaughan.............	11
Did not life's darkness dim our sight........	Potters American Monthly.	33
Down to the borders of the silent land.......·..................	Washington Gladden........	13˙
Earth with its dark and dreadful ills..........................	Alice Cary.................	268
Eternal spirit of the chainless mind......................	Byron....	120
Ever and ever the world goes round		175
Every day is a fresh beginning...	Susan Coolidge.............	53
Fasten your soul so high that constantly..................	E. B. Browning	105
Father! I must lean hard......		215
Forgive! that oft my spirit wears.	Angelus Silesius	167
Fret not thyself so sorely, heart of mine....................		90
From the mountain-side of years.	A. P. Miller	193
Give strength whene'er our strength must fail...	Marperger..	66
Go breathe it in the ear.........	Longfellow.................	128
God keeps a niche in heaven.....	E. B. Browning.......... .	235
God lifts the soul or casts it down.	A. P. Miller.......	49
God liveth ever...	Zihn	72
God plumeth many a spirit.......	Mrs. A. D. T. Whitney	115

	AUTHOR.	PAGE.
God's justice is a bed, where we.		85
Go not far in the land of light...	Alice Cary	254
Good night! good night! as we so oft have said	Longfellow	242
Good night my foe! not all the wrong is thine	Harriet McEwen Kimball...	91
Great God, we know not what we know	Alice Cary	27
Great truths are greatly won, not found by chance	Horatius Bonar	63
Gropest thou in failure's valley?.		82
Groping blindly in the darkness..	Longfellow	17
Happiest man among men	MacCarthy	100
Hark! the stars are talking	Geo. Macdonald	3
Having won by toil and pain.		176
Heart, my heart be strong	A. Werner	87
He does well. who does his best..		276
"Heimgang!" so the German people say		156
He is the freeman who the truth makes free	Cowper	118
He looks abroad into the varied field	Cowper	103
He who died at Azan sends.	Edwin Arnold	229
Hide thee awhile, call back the troublous past	Amelia E. Barr	191
Homeward the swift-winged sea-gull takes its flight		119
Hope in our souls is king	Longfellow	118
How dark this world would be...	Thomas More	94
How many of us have ships at sea.	Florence Grover	184
How shalt thou bear the cross that now	Faber	84
Humility is the base of every virtue	Bailey	85
I am going away, dear friend....	Susan Archer Weiss	261
I cannot see with my small human sight		19
I do not know the deadly depths within	M. Woolsey Stryker	66
If as we dream in every radiant star	N. P. Willis	255
If by our toil another's feet may rise	Laura B. Boyce	104
If for a time some loved one goes away	A. D. F. Randolph	233

	AUTHOR.	PAGE.
If I must win my way to perfectness....	J. G. Holland	211
If indeed	Thomas Burbidge. .	18
If thou impatient do let slip thy cross	Ugo Bassi's Sermon.	222
If you sit down at set of sun		181
I have a little trembling light, which still.	Henry Septimus Sutton.	23
I have a sin of fear	Bishop Donne	137
I have borne scorn and hatred....		86
I have no moan to make	Phoebe Cary	240
I have some songs I do not sing..	Samuel Duffield.	210
I hear a voice ye cannot hear....	Tickell	266
I heard the trailing garments of the Night	Longfellow..	10
I know a dark and lonely dell....	James Buckham	117
I know not what the future hath..	Whittier	138
I know not where thine islands lift	Whittier	276
I know the hand that is guiding me	British Evangelist	28
I know thy wondrous ways will end		206
I mind the weary days of old.,...	A. D. F. Randolph	197
In a far away land on a stone it is written		90
In dreams that hold.	F. W. Bourdillon	194
In God I'll trust		35
In my right hand I clasp to-morrow's grief	Anna Temple	55
In Poverty's dark cell I sit		108
In the dusk of our sorrowful hours	Margaret E. Sangster	50
In the throng	J. G. Holland	65
In this cruel fire of sorrow... ...	Frances Ridley Havergal ..	93
In weariness I wait and pray		120
I remember best	Amelia E. Barr	45
I said one day, O life ! you're little worth.	Laura Garland Carr. .	164
I sit beside the sea	Edna Dean Proctor	244
I sit upon a cypress bough	E. B. Browning	113
Is not the night all dark. A. W. in	"Cambridge Review."	121
Is thy cruise of comfort failing?..	Mrs. Charles	45
I think we are too ready with complaint	E. B. Browning	43
I thought to work for Him.		214
It is one thing to be tempted.....	Shakespeare...	75
I tremble at the thought of heaven	Ella M. Baker	134
I trust in my soul.	Owen Meredith	205

AUTHOR.   PAGE.

I trust Thee, O Father, Thy word can not fail........... Mrs. L. S. Mills.. 32
It sometimes happens....... ... Sunday Afternoon 242
It was a day of darkness and of doubt.......... .... A. P. Miller.. 28
I wait..... .... Mary Clemmer..... 207
I walk down the Valley of Silence. Father Ryan................ 175
I was sitting alone in the twilight. Mrs. Herrick Johnson....... 152
I will go forth among men, not mailed in scorn.............. Alexander Smith............ 81
I would be joyful as my days go by........... .... A. D. F. Randolph.......... 20

Known only, only to God....... Alfred H. Louis............. 15
Know that his dear children cannot die..................... 232

Labor ! all labor is noble and holy. Frances S. Osgood....... ... 105
Laborare est orare.......... .... Miss Mulock............... 102
Late on me weeping did this whisper fall.... .... Henry Septimus Sutton... .. 60
Leave God to order all thy ways. George Newman........... 133
Let us be like the bird. Victor Hugo, translated by.......... Edwin Arnold 130
Let us be patient with our lot.... Josiah Moody Fletcher...... 100
Life we have been long together. Mrs. Barbauld..... 274
Like a thorn in the flesh, like a fly in the mesh .... Ella Wheeler......... 56
Lo ! amid the press.......... . . Susan Coolidge 148
Look above thee. never eye...... Bowring...................... 265
Lord, according to Thy words.... George Macdonald.......... 170
"Lord, a little, little longer !".... Miss Mulock......... 223
Lord, be mine this prize to win.. H. F. Lyte 72
Lord, if I dip my cup into the sea. 150
Lo ! the marvelous contrast of shadow and light .... Edward Dean Rand.... 13

My heart grows strong.... .... . Duke of Brunswick.... ... 67
My soul complaineth not......... Winkler... 18
My wine has run indeed out of my cup.......... ... . E. B. Browning. 104

'Neath some shadow oft I wait.... John Ordronaux 68
Never on the clear bright billow.. Augusta Harvey Worthen.. 69
Never think of me as lying....... Phœbe Cary 276
No bird-song floated down the hill...................... .. ...Whittier 215
No evil ! But behold, how tempest tost !.......... .... S. W. Weitzel............... 14
No light ! we say....... ... . Edmund C. Stedman........ 29
No strain..... 200

	AUTHOR.	PAGE.
Not all who seem to fail have failed indeed		105
Not in vain do we	Frances L. Mace	275
Not so hopeless, drooping spirit	Horatius Bonar	45
Not to forget when pain and grief draw nigh	Henry Septimus Sutton	201
Not yet, O friend! not yet	Bret Harte	9
Now I need not fear for thee	Paul Gerhardt	238
O black and bitter night	Adelaide George Bennett	24
O, don't be sorrowful, darling	Rembrandt Peale	17
O God, O kinsman loved, but not enough	Jean Ingelow	74
Oh! blessed are the dead	Eliza Mary Hamilton	249
Oh deem not they are blessed alone	Bryant	86
Oh, our Father, our Father. A. Werner in "The King of the Silver City."		121
Oh, the temple of the soul, of what tiny stones 'tis built		174
Oh! tried heart	Mabel ——	93
Oh weary heart of the toiler	William Byrd Chrisholm	101
Oh, what will be that life to come?	G. W. Crofts	270
O little bird! that all the weary day	Ada Gale	116
O Memory, ope thy mystic door	David Gray	199
On a far shore, my land swam far from my sight		274
Once in the twilight of a wintry day	Emily Huntingdon Miller	237
Once pain beat upon my heart	Ella Wheeler	208
One day at a time! every heart that beats	Helen Jackson (H. H.)	156
One of these days it will all be over		185
One summer day to a young child I said		147
On every morrow are we wreathing	Keats	49
Open the Western Gate	Amelia E. Barr	143
O soul of mine, when tasks are hard and long		59
O sudden blast, that through this silence black	Miss Mulock	217
Our course is onward, onward into light	Trench	46
Our prince has gone to his inheritance	Julia C. R. Dorr	232
Our very perils shut us in	Anna Letitia Waring	130

	AUTHOR.	PAGE.
Out of the sunshine warm and soft and bright.............. ..	Anon....................	30
Over the narrow foot-path.	Margaret E. Sangster.	158
Over us, patient and changeless and far.	Frances L Mace.........	13
O weary hearts that languish....	Adelaide George Bennett....	48
Pain's furnace heat within me quivers..................	....	220
Plan not, nor scheme, but calmly wait.................	Macduff....................	128
Raise it to heaven when thine eye fills with tears.....	Frances Kemble Butler.....	55
Reach down the wanderer's staff.	Frances Kemble Butler.....	267
Restless, restless speed we on....	William C. Gannett........	22
Rise up, sad one, and outward cast........................ ..	Adelaide George Bennett....	26
Roll on, O earth! roll on and swing..................... .	Edwin S. Hopkins..........	61
Saying "There is no hope," he stepped...................... ...	Elizabeth Stuart Phelps.....	252
See how the far east brightens!..	Tr. from Fouqué by Andrews	260
Seek not to know.................	....	27
See the Lord, thy keeper, stand..	Charles Wesley..	137
Serene I fold my hands and wait.	John Burroughs........ ..	148
Shall one who does God's image bear.....................	A.J. S.in N. Hampshire Poets	106
Shall we sit idly down. From "Morituri Salutamus" .. .	Longfellow.............. ..	186
She said I am come to heaven at last.....	Elizabeth Stuart Phelps.....	264
She shut the door and turned away........	..........................···	254
Should bereavement's heavy shadow.......................	....	232
Shut in with tears that are spent in vain..................	. ...	123
Silence and darkness, solitude and sorrow..	....	22
Softly sing the love of Jesus......	....	82
So let us die	....	265
Some comfort when all else is night........................	Alice Cary	200
Some day or other I shall surely come	Louise Chandler Moulton...	172
Some souls cut off from moorings ...	....	36
Sometimes I am tempted to murmur.........	Margaret E. Sangster.	160

	AUTHOR.	PAGE.
Sorely tried and sorely tempted.. From " Masque of Pandora".	Longfellow....	74
Sorrow and silence are strong.... From "Evangeline".........	Longfellow	115
Souls that of his own good life partake......................	Henry More....	238
Speak to us out of midnight's heart	Lucy Larcom in "January "	12
Still alway groweth in me the great wonder...............	Alice Cary...	250
Strange, strange for thee and me.	Phœbe Cary...	253
Strong are the mountains, Lord, but stronger Thou.....	....	129
Summer days.....	".B. M."...................	194
Sum up at night what thou hast done by day...........	George Herbert........	192
Take unto thyself, O Father.....	....	54
Tempted in all points like our-selves	J. G. Holland.	77
Tears are not always fruitful.....	Horatius Bonar	59
Thanks for the benediction of thy love......	Hester M. Poole...	187
The birds have hushed their chorus.....................	A. M. in the "Quiver ". ...	13
The Border lands are calm and still...	....	207
The child leans on its mother's breast..........	....	21
The clouds may rest on the present...................	Phœbe Cary............. .,....	39
The coiled elastic spring of steel.	E. E. Adams...	168
The cup of my years was filling..	J. H. M....	161
" The days are all alike " she said	....	182
The earth, O prisoned soul, is thine.............................	.. ..	120
The faint, low echo that we hear.	Adelaide A. Proctor...	184
The hands are such dear hands...	N. Y. Independent	157
The happy dreams that gladdened all our youth.....................	....	199
The heart grows richer that its lot is poor.................... ...	Lowell	106
The helper of his mother ..:.....	M. Woolsey Stryker.........	99
The little flowers breathe sweet-ness out...	Sarah Williams.............	23
The Lord knoweth when each hot tear floweth	G. Z. G......................	219
The Master e'er His work was done....	Mrs. Luther Keene..	109
The moon was pallid but not faint.............	Longfellow....	87

	AUTHOR.	PAGE.
The night is come; like to the day	Sir Thomas Browne	163
The past is mine and I take it all.	Phœbe Cary	75
There is a grandeur in the soul that dares	Sara J. Clarke	128
There is always sunrise some-where		46
There is no soul but has some deep regret	A. P. Miller	197
There's many a rest on the road of life		183
There's not an hour but from some sparkling beach	Helen Jackson (H. H.)	255
There was a time when meadow, grove and stream	Wordsworth	195
The same old baffling questions	Whittier	206
The sands of time are sinking		272
These saddened years	W. R. Cochrane	47
The shady nooks and corners	Margeret E. Sangster	172
The stars are in the sky all day	Susan Coolidge	39
The sudden joys that out of dark-ness start	Longfellow	198
The sufferer sings—his end is near..Tr. from Schmolke by.	Gurney	275
The things over which we grieved with lashes wet		192
The waves they are wildly heav-ing	Alice Cary	259
The way is long, my darling	Margaret E. Sangster	179
They are poor that have lost nothing	Jean Ingelow	132
They never quite leave us	Margaret E. Sangster	247
They only the victory win.		71
They who have learned to pray aright		207
Think ye the notes of holy song..	Whittier	195
This leaf, this stone, it is thy heart		205
This shall please Thee, if devoutly trying	Johann Heerman	67
Thou art my God	Henry Septimus Sutton	37
Thou who hast so long pressed the couch of pain	Bryant	224
Through black waves and stormy blast	Susan Coolidge	21
Thy gifts sustain	Christian Register	104
Tired? Well, what of that?		58
'Tis all I have—smoke, failure, foiled endeavor	George Macdonald	81
'Tis the bold who win the race		127
Tossed on temptation's sea		76

AUTHOR.   PAGE.

Turn the Past's mirror backward. Miss Mulock............... 273

Unto Him who washed us... ..... B. M........ 267
Unto the hills I lift mine eyes. 124
Upon the sadness of the sea...... R. W. M.................... 5
Up, up, the day is breaking....   Paul Gerhardt.............   21

Vital spark of heavenly flame !... Alexander Pope············ 269

We are waiting, Father, waiting   Hayes C. French...........   33
We ask Thy peace, O Lord !..... Adelaide A. Proctor........   96
We, ignorant of ourselves....... Shakespeare................   49
We need not die to go to God.... 166
Were there no night we could not
    read the stars.............. ...... Henry Burton......... 119
We see by night's sweet showing. Alex. R. Thompson........   10
We shall be like Him, strange the
    story.............. .... Harriet Chase.... 165
We shall not die until our work
    be done................. 157
We should live as if expecting... Josiah Moody Fletcher...... 144
What a strange Being holds me in
    his might.................. .... Charlotte Fiske Bates... ... 139
Whate'er God does is well..... .. Schmolke. 106
What else remains for me?...... 84
What foe can injure me?......... Lyte...................... 129
What is that we call death?...... Increase N. Tarbox......... 266
What matter how the winds may
    blow................... .... A. D. F. Randolph.......... 151
What profit to lay on God's altar. Margaret J. Preston........ 212
What tears in your eyes, my
    beloved ! .... Mabel ——.. 161
What though before me it is dark. British Messengers......... 31
What though the web our hands
    shall leave undone.......... Laura B. Boyce 211
What though we grope and
    stumble in the way.......... Laura B. Boyce............. 66
What to shut eyes has God re-
    vealed?...................... Whittier 243
When all the weary toil with
    which we wrought........ .. Laura B. Boyce............. 85
When doomed to feel that youth
    is o'er.... 201
When sins and follies long forgot 130
When sorrow's darkest night.... Julia D. Peck.............. 163
When the sad soul in weariness.. Joseph W. Sutphen.... 83
When the song's gone out of your
    life........................ 44
When you see a soul set free..... Phœbe Cary............... 233
Whether winds blow foul or fair. 108
Why art thou full of anxious fear. Paul Gerhardt............. 108

	AUTHOR.	PAGE.
Why forecast the trials of life....		180
Why should we do ourselves this wrong.................		147
Why that look of dark dismay ?..	Arthur C. Grisson...........	138
Why weep ye for the falling.....	Alice Cary.................	277
Will it be always night?.......	Nettie Vernon..............	29
Workman of God, Oh, lose not heart........................	"Songs of Devotion".......	127
Would that I too were lying.....	Jean Ingelow..............	246
You have said that God is just...	J. G. Holland...	38

www.ingramcontent.com/pod-product-compliance
Lightning Source LLC
Chambersburg PA
CBHW021218270326
41929CB00010B/1182